Theology
from the Trenches

Theology
from the Trenches

Reflections on Urban Ministry

ROGER J. GENCH

WESTMINSTER
JOHN KNOX PRESS
LOUISVILLE · KENTUCKY

First Edition
Published by Westminster John Knox Press
Louisville, Kentucky

14 15 16 17 18 19 20 21 22 23—10 9 8 7 6 5 4 3 2 1

Book design by Sharon Adams
Cover design by Dilu Nicholas
Cover illustration: Asphalt Background with danger signs
© Krivosheev Vitaly/shutterstock.com;
Prague, Czech Republic—December 11: The Lennon Wall/Image ID 67118314
© Emka74/shutterstock.com

Library of Congress Cataloging-in-Publication Data

Gench, Roger J.
  Theology from the trenches : reflections on urban ministry / Roger J. Gench.—First edition.
    pages cm
  ISBN 978-0-664-23968-8 (alk. paper)
  1. City churches. 2. Church work. 3. Christian communities. 4. City missions. 5. Jesus Christ—Crucifixion. I. Title.
  BV637.G46 2014
  250.9173'2—dc23

2014004505

∞ The paper used in this publication meets the minimum requirements
of the American National Standard for Information Sciences—Permanence
of Paper for Printed Library Materials, ANSI Z39.48-1992.

Most Westminster John Knox Press books are available at special quantity discounts
when purchased in bulk by corporations, organizations, and special-interest groups.
For more information, please e-mail SpecialSales@wjkbooks.com.

Contents

Acknowledgments

I am greatly indebted to the leadership and members of the Brown Memorial Park Avenue Presbyterian Church in Baltimore, Maryland, and The New York Avenue Presbyterian Church in Washington, D.C., because most of the material in this book emerged from shared ministry with them in these two urban contexts. I wish to offer a special word of thanks to the session of The New York Avenue Presbyterian Church for granting me a sabbatical leave that made it possible for me to finish this project.

I also thank my colleagues Kathleen O'Toole, Jonathan Lange, Arnie Graf, Coleman Milling, Rob English, Martin Trimble, and Amy Vruno, who work as organizers for the Industrial Areas Foundation; they have taught me the tools of community organizing and much about life in the city. Their energy and spirit has always been an inspiration to me.

The original draft of chapter 1 was presented to fellow participants in a year-long seminar on race and the Reformed Tradition at Union Presbyterian Seminary in Richmond, Virginia, led by Professors Katie Cannon and Sam Roberts. I wish to thank Katie and Sam for this formative learning experience and for their support and feedback—and because the writing of this essay on the closing of an inner city grocery store prompted me to write this book on urban ministry.

I am grateful for my colleagues in ministry at The New York Avenue Presbyterian Church and for their partnership in many of the initiatives described in this book—Tara Spuhler McCabe (my ministry teammate for a decade), Linda Lader, and Katie Cashwell. I also thank Lionel Edmonds, Joe Daniels, Doug Miles, Curtis Jones, Jeff Krehbiel, and Karen Brau—my colleagues in the two affiliate organizations of the Industrial Areas Foundation that have played such an important role in my engagement with urban ministry: Baltimoreans United in Leadership Development and the Washington Interfaith Network. I specifically thank Kathleen O'Toole and Jeff Krehbiel for reminding me of the importance of using community organizing tools for organizing the church.

I am most grateful to Paul Dornan for carefully reading the manuscript and providing helpful feedback. I will always be indebted to my mentor, Charlie Swezey, and am especially grateful for important conversations with him about H. Richard Niebuhr's *Christ and Culture* (though any errors in my presentation of Niebuhr are mine, not his). I am indebted to David Dobson, David Maxwell, and Daniel Braden, my editors at Westminster John Knox Press, for their many insightful suggestions for improving this book.

Finally I thank my wife, Frances Taylor Gench, for her unflagging support of this project and constructive editorial assistance; I doubt that I would have finished this book without her encouragement.

I dedicate this book, with deep gratitude, to the members and ministries of The New York Avenue Presbyterian Church, God's "Salt and Light" in the nation's capital.

Introduction

Urban congregations devote time, energy, and attention to all the basic demands of church life, such as budgets, building and maintenance, personnel issues, and the worship, education, and nurture of its members. But urban congregations committed to ministry in their context also grapple with formidable issues endemic to city life: homelessness, scarcity of living wage jobs, racism, mental illness, crime, and educational and economic disparities. Any one of these issues could completely absorb the time, energy, and attention of a dedicated congregation, and achieving a measure of balance amid competing demands and responsibilities is daunting. I offer this book in hopes of helping pastors and congregants (and those who aspire to urban ministry) access theological, relational, and spiritual resources that can sustain ministry in challenging urban contexts.

I have spent the better part of the last three decades in the trenches of urban ministry. The word "trench" no doubt conveys that I have found it to be a demanding vocation—and there is no question about that! Urban areas are afflicted by a range of distinctive predicaments with which urban churches contend. But when I speak of the "trenches of urban ministry," know that there is nowhere else that I would rather be. Actually, I did not set out in this direction at the start of my journey. Initially, I thought I wanted to teach theology and ethics, and thus I pursued, and eventually attained, the requisite academic degree. Due to job scarcity in the academic world, I backed my way into the parish where, much to my surprise, I found my vocation. The parish—and the trenches of urban ministry in particular—turned out to be for me the best possible place to engage theology and ethics with authenticity, a place where theology and ethics made a real difference in human lives. Much to my surprise, I found that I loved teaching, preaching, and talking theology, day in and day out, in the parish, with people whom I discovered were yearning to learn about the Christian faith, many of whom had been drawn to

1

urban churches because they also wanted to take ethics by the horns and do something about the plights of urban areas to contribute in some way to the mending of creation. They were interested in what was being taught in our seminaries and found it relevant for their lives and wanted to put their faith into practice. Thus I found my calling and have been passionate ever since about bridging the world of the academy and the parish, bringing the living faith of the Christian tradition to bear on the life and practices of the church. The primary impetus for this book is to share some of that with you—to reflect on doing theology from the trenches of urban ministry.

I believe that doing theology in the life of the church, and helping others do the same, is vital to the practice of ministry, and I hope to make that case in the pages that follow. Two other endeavors have been integral to my experience of the trenches of urban ministry—and sometimes to my survival in the midst of it—and need to be mentioned at the outset, because they inform the reflection that follows in significant ways. One is community organizing, and the other is practice of the contemplative arts. I "cut my teeth" in urban ministry through community organizing. For those unfamiliar with this term, "community organizing" simply refers to folks organized to act on their self-interest. The Industrial Areas Foundation, an organization that was founded in the 1940s, is now the nation's largest and oldest network of faith- and community-based organizations. As its website explains, it "partners with religious congregations and civic organizations at the local level to build broad-based organizing projects, which create new capacity in a community for leadership development, citizen-led action and relationships across the lines that often divide our communities."[1] For the past twenty-four years, I have served on the clergy leadership teams of two IAF affiliates (in Baltimore, Maryland, and Washington, D.C.), and consequently community organizing is in my blood and has played a formative role in my practice of urban ministry. It has taught me a great deal about the power of relational culture—the power of connecting deeply with people's stories of anger over injustices and their yearning to do something about it. I have found that the tools of community organizing are not only an effective way to organize a local community but have a great deal to contribute to the life and ministry of the church as well. Throughout my engagement and my congregations' engagements with local IAF organizations, I have been convinced that the tools of relational organizing touch something very deep and essential in Christian faith and theology. I have thought long and hard about the connections between the two and do not shy away from bringing the tools of community organizing into a transformational conversation with my faith. And in this volume I hope to share some of that reflection as well, in hopes that it will provide food for thought.

The other integral aspect of my life in urban ministry has been the contemplative, or what others might refer to as engagement with spiritual disciplines, and this too will be reflected in this volume. For the last twenty years, I have been a devotee of the contemplative arts—prayer and meditation of varied sorts. They have played a vital role in my own life of faith, and I am convinced that they are vital also to the life and ministry of an urban congregation. Facilitating and nurturing congregational engagement with contemplative practices thus have played an increasingly important role in my ministry, and this practice is central to my own understanding of my pastoral vocation. The contemplative arts are essential to discernment of what God is calling a congregation to be and do and are a wellspring for a congregation's engagement with the world. They enable us to grow more fully into the love of God and neighbor to which the Great Commandment calls us. I hope to share something of the role contemplation has played in my own life and that of my urban congregation and prompt reflection on this front as well.

One other matter needs to be addressed at the outset, a touchstone for the road ahead as we reflect on urban ministry. Let me introduce what has become for me the guiding symbol or metaphor for my understanding of urban ministry.

The Cruciform Covenant

I love cities and have lived in urban areas of varied sizes almost all of my life. I have often pondered the symbols used to capture their life and vitality. For example, the official website of Baltimore, where I resided for twelve years, contains a picture of the city skyline above the waters of the Inner Harbor—the city's historic seaport and central landmark. It has played a vital role in the city's economic history, as a seaport for ships that traveled up the Chesapeake Bay from the Atlantic, and more recently as a model of urban renaissance, as the waterfront has been transformed with parks, plazas, corporate office spaces, hotels, and tourist attractions. Civic symbols are even more prominent and pervasive in Washington, where I currently reside. As the nation's capital, it is filled with iconic governmental buildings, monuments, and museums. However, Washington's dominant symbol is without a doubt the U.S. Capitol building, which sits atop Capitol Hill at the east end of the National Mall. It is D.C.'s chief economic engine, the hub of its life. However, both of these landmarks, in Baltimore and Washington, are flawed in important respects as symbols of civic vitality, because the economies of these two cities have never served all their residents well—a reality reflected in all major urban areas throughout the country. Other powerful symbols of modern metropolitan life also fail to represent and deliver vitality and fullness of life for all urban dwellers. The skyscraper (or the skyline) is called into question by the pervasive reality of inner-city slums. Factories and smokestacks were once symbols of urban industrial strength, but globalization (and the loss of jobs) and environmental abuses have rendered these symbols defunct. A fully promising symbol for the modern city is hard to come by.

I've been in search of one that would capture for my urban congregations the ministry to which God calls us in the city. I've long been intrigued by the fact that the Bible's culminating vision of the future that God has in mind for us is an urban one—a vision of a new heaven and a new earth, and of "the holy city, the new Jerusalem, coming down out of heaven from God" (Rev. 21:2), in which God will dwell among mortals. The biblical vision of the new Jerusalem is an inspiring one for urban ministry in many respects, as we will note in the chapters to follow, but there can be no denying that the history of its interpretation has been deeply problematic. Indeed, the symbol of the new Jerusalem (along with a cluster of related metaphors, such as the "new Israel" or "the elect") was deployed by early Americans to express their belief that they were a chosen people with a special destiny—a belief used to justify the exclusion of others (such as Native Americans and slaves) from God's covenant.[2] Abraham Lincoln was acutely aware of this ambiguous history. In fact, en route to Washington, D.C., after his election, in a whistle-stop speech, Lincoln provided an alternative description of Americans as an "almost chosen people."[3] In other words, he seemed to have misgivings about any presumption on our part of a special American destiny. When Lincoln was president, he attended The New York Avenue Presbyterian Church, where I currently serve as senior pastor, and where his pew, his memory, and his wisdom are esteemed. Thus I have taken his description of Americans as "almost chosen people" as cautionary wisdom in my search for an appropriate symbol for urban ministry, one that can embrace the ambiguous, broken dimensions of human reality and that of the communities around us. So, let me propose what I hope will capture for urban Christians the nature of the ministry to which God calls us in the city. I believe that God calls us to embody a "cruciform covenant." Why have I proposed a "cruciform (or cross-shaped) covenant" as a symbol that can speak powerfully to urban Christians, providing vision for our ministry?

Let me begin with the notion of *cruciformity*. It is a central concept that will surface at points throughout the book, and I realize it is one to which some readers may have an instinctive aversion. Thus it is important for me to say what cruciformity conveys in my view—and perhaps more importantly, what it does not. I do not have in mind any notion of placating the wrath of an angry God through the sacrifice of an innocent victim (Christ)—the so-called satisfaction or penal substitution view of atonement. I could not agree more with theologian Serene Jones who says this about traditional interpretations of the cross: "When I consider the many ways theologians interpret the cross, I strongly reject any aspect of a theology of the cross that turns God into an intentional agent of traumatic violence, and I firmly believe that however one interprets it, the crucifixion both denounces evil and also announces the universal reality of divine love, of grace."[4]

So what *do* I have in mind when I use the descriptive "cruciform" or reference "cruciformity"? In Ernest Hemingway's novel *A Farewell to Arms,* a character says that "the world breaks everyone and afterward many are strong in the broken places."[5] Let me paraphrase these words to define "cruciformity": *The world crucifies everyone, yet God in Christ is always and already active in the world, bringing life out of the broken places.* Thus there are two dimensions of cruciformity: it encompasses both crucifixion and resurrection.

First, when I speak of crucifixion, I am referring of course to an historical reality but also to what I believe is a symbol for the abuse of power. The historical reality is that Jesus was crucified, and his crucifixion was an instrument of state terrorism that the Roman Empire used to force their colonies into submission. (In today's military jargon, we might speak of this display of power in terms of "shock and awe.") Crucifixion thus can also be a symbol for any exercise of power, however large or small, that dominates, deforms, or defaces human life or God's good creation, because such power mimics the power that crucified Jesus. For example, as we look at the world through the lens of the cross, it exposes the many crucifixions happening all around us in the urban environment—points at which human life and God's creation suffer as a result of economic injustice and classism, ethnocentrism and racism, segregation and hyper-segregation of inner-city neighborhoods, environmental degradation, sexism, heterosexism, greed, hatred, or self-hatred. In what sense is racism, economic injustice, or segregation crucifying powers? Because in each case power is used to dominate, deform, or deface some in order to benefit others or to keep oppressed people in their place. Moreover, passivity in the face of deforming conditions to which racism or injustice give rise (as they are manifested, for example, in joblessness, underperforming schools, absence of medical care or affordable housing) is itself a kind of crucifying power, because passivity and neglect (sins of omission) enable crucifixions to endure through time. So when I interpret the cross,

I use the language of "exposure" or exposé to convey the symbolic power of the cross of Jesus as a lens that enables us to see other crosses, large and small, that litter both our external and internal landscapes. [6]

In addition, the theology of the cross of which I speak in this book is grounded in "political theology." The word "political" comes from the Greek word *polis*, which means "city." As theologian Elizabeth Johnson explains, political theology is "theology that seeks to connect speech about God with the *polis*, the city, the public good of massive numbers of people, living and dead."[7] A political theology of the cross seeks to expose sin (such as those mentioned above) that is both public (in our urban environment) and internalized or inscribed upon us; and it directs our attention to ways in which we tend to reinscribe sin onto the world around us. Ted Jennings offers a particularly astute summary of the politics of the cross. The cross, he says, is a collision between the way of Jesus and the politics of domination. This collision is unavoidable, and God wills that the roots of suffering and abuse be "exposed" and brought to an end.[8] He continues:

> One way that this is expressed in the tradition is that God comes in Christ in order to overcome sin. The end of sin is the end of this game of violence, of collaboration in violence, of imitation of violence—a violence exercised in the name of the supposedly "strong God" it imitates. It is because of "our sin," as Paul suggests, that the Messiah is repudiated, condemned, and executed. *But this does not mean because of a long list of personal sins. It has rather to do with our participation in a world that rules by and collaborates in violence, exclusion, and judgment. This is the pervasive reality in which we are caught up.* It plays out in our relationships with people we "love," as well as our relationships with our "enemies." It plays out in relationship of the elite to those they control. But it also plays out among the excluded—not in the same way, but in ways that still mirror the deadly force of domination and division, even when this or that element of oppression is actively opposed. It is this scene of violence and violation that is entered by the messianic mission, and it is from this same dynamic that this mission suffers and dies.[9]

Note the way in which Jennings uses language of exposure to speak of the cross. He claims that at its most basic level, the cross "strips the powers of domination and violence of their pretended legitimacy" and reveals God's solidarity with the "oppressed and humiliated."[10] So the cross both "unmasks" and "reveals"—it unmask domination's pretension to power and reveals God's sovereign and cruciform covenant love.

The "revealing" power of cruciformity is critically important, for if the cross exposes sin, it also discloses the God who is always and already bringing life out of the death-tending ways of our world. Or as Nadia Bolz-Weber has put it, "God keeps reaching down into the dirt of humanity and resurrecting us from the graves we dig for ourselves through our violence, our lies, our selfishness, our arrogance and our addictions. And God keeps loving us back to life over and over."[11] The profound affirmation of cruciform faith is that God refuses to give up on God's creation and is at every moment bringing life or resurrection out of the crucified places of our world. Here I am drawn to Elizabeth Johnson's image for the cross. She speaks of the crucified and risen Christ as the "lens" through which we interpret the living God in our midst. Through this lens "we glimpse a merciful love that knows no bounds. Jesus' ministry . . . made the love of God experientially available to all, the marginalized most of all."[12] In sum, cruciformity encompasses both crucifixion and resurrection, for God is at work in the world to bring life out of broken places.

In a recent conversation, a member of my church captured "cruciformity" in a striking and lucid fashion, I thought, when he called attention to both the horizontal and vertical dimensions of the cross. He observed that the horizontal bar of the cross represents the ways in which the fear, violence, and death preoccupy and oppress our lives, while the vertical bar represents the ways in which God is intersecting our death-preoccupied lives in order to bring resurrection and life. I believe that our task as urban Christians is to stand at those places of intersection. Dietrich Bonhoeffer, in his struggle against Nazi tyranny, put it this way: "The reality of God discloses itself only by setting me entirely in the reality of the world; but there I find the reality of the world always already created, sustained, judged, and reconciled in the reality of God."[13]

Practically speaking, what might standing at such an intersection look like? The Community Club program at the church I currently serve in Washington is an example of how a congregation can stand at an intersection where God is bringing life out of broken places. Among the crosses that litter many urban landscapes are the failures of inner-city schools to provide an adequate education for their students, and D.C.'s public school system is ranked among the worst in the nation. But every Thursday night for the last 50 years, some 100 to 125 students (grades 7–12) from the D.C. public school system come to the church for tutoring in every subject to meet with 100 to 125 tutors from the city who are involved in this program. Students and tutors are partnered one-on-one with each other in a relationship that extends through the course of the student's high school education. And every year, the graduation rate for these high school seniors is nearly 100 percent; most have been accepted on scholarship to colleges and universities. These graduates move on to become entrepreneurs, educators, and good citizens. Students and tutors alike testify to the life-giving covenants, or deep relationships, that they form with each other—relationships that in many cases endure for a lifetime.

I hope this elaboration has clarified the sense in which I will be using the term "cruciformity." But the metaphor I am proposing for urban ministry is "cruciform *covenant*," so what about that second term? This, too, needs elaboration, for the word "covenant" captures a crucial dimension of God's relationship with the world, as well as a crucial dimension of our own engagement in urban ministry. A "covenant" is a binding and unconditional commitment. God's covenant with the world is the premier expression of this commitment. And I contend that cruciformity best describes the trajectory of God's covenant with the world. Consider, for example, Isaiah 61, in which this trajectory finds expression in a message to Israelites returning to the devastated city Jerusalem from exile in Babylon:

> The spirit of the Lord GOD is upon me,
>   because the LORD has anointed me;
> he has sent me to bring good news to the oppressed,
>   to bind up the brokenhearted,
> to proclaim liberty to the captives,
>   and release to the prisoners;
> to proclaim the year of the LORD's favor,
>   and the day of vengeance of our God;
>   to comfort all who mourn;
> to provide for those who mourn in Zion—
>   to give them a garland instead of ashes,
> the oil of gladness instead of mourning,
>   the mantle of praise instead of a faint spirit.
> They will be called oaks of righteousness,
>   the planting of the LORD, to display his glory.
> They shall build up the ancient ruins,
>   they shall raise up the former devastations;
> they shall repair the ruined cities,
>   the devastations of many generations.
>
> Strangers shall stand and feed your flocks,
>   foreigners shall till your land and dress your vines;
> but you shall be called priests of the LORD,
>   you shall be named ministers of our God;
> you shall enjoy the wealth of the nations,
>   and in their riches you shall glory.
> Because their shame was double,
>   and dishonor was proclaimed as their lot,

therefore they shall possess a double portion;
    everlasting joy shall be theirs.

For I the LORD love justice,
    I hate robbery and wrongdoing;
I will faithfully give them their recompense,
    and I will make an everlasting covenant with them.
Their descendants shall be known among the nations,
    and their offspring among the peoples;
all who see them shall acknowledge
    that they are a people whom the LORD has blessed.
I will greatly rejoice in the LORD,
    my whole being shall exult in my God;
for he has clothed me with the garments of salvation,
    he has covered me with the robe of righteousness,
as a bridegroom decks himself with a garland,
    and as a bride adorns herself with her jewels.
For as the earth brings forth its shoots,
    and as a garden causes what is sown in it to spring up,
so the Lord GOD will cause righteousness and praise
    to spring up before all the nations.

This passage provides an inspiring vision for urban ministry, for in it the prophet Isaiah proclaims God's everlasting covenant and promised renewal of the devastated city so that the divine glory will be revealed. The returning exiles are given the privilege of participating in God's salvific work of rebuilding and repair: *"They shall build up the ancient ruins, they shall raise up the former devastations; they shall repair the ruined cities, the devastations of many generations"* (v. 4). Moreover, the revived community will be one in which the poor will see God reverse their fortunes, for injustice insults the creator of a just world. This message would be good news to many of the residents of America's urban areas, who find themselves exiled from the full and abundant life that is God's will for all people.

The covenantal vision that Isaiah projects can be located on a trajectory that I would describe as "cruciform" or cross-shaped, for it clearly springs from broken, devastated places and moves outward toward justice and restored blessing for all. Indeed, implicit in the covenant Isaiah envisions is the whole sweep of the biblical story of God's covenant-making with Israel—which begins with Noah and his descendants (the initial recipients of God's "everlasting covenant") and moves steadily outward as the covenant people journey through slavery, exile, and return. In the New Testament, Jesus embraces Isaiah's vision (see Luke 4:16–19) as a programmatic statement of the nature and course of his whole ministry, and Paul's mission extends the covenant promise in ever widening circles as he takes the gospel of Christ crucified to Gentiles. From beginning to end, God's everlasting covenant embraces the marginal, the enslaved, the exiled, a crucified and risen Messiah, and moves outward to bless an exiled and broken world. In other words, God's covenant – the trajectory of God's work in the world—is cross-shaped, which is to say that it springs from broken places, bringing justice, resurrection and life out of a death-tending world.

If God's way in the world can be described as cruciform and covenantal, so can the ministry to which we are summoned in urban settings. For urban churches are called to covenant with God and others at the intersection of the places where God is bringing life out to the death-tending ways of our urban realities. In his insightful book on urban ministry, Ronald Peters identified these death-tending realities as alienation, fear, and violence. What he notes is that cities, while more pluralistic than their suburban counterparts, tend to respond to differences in class, race, and ethnicity with segregation. This response is prompted by fear of the "other," who is labeled as immigrant, criminal, or a threat of some sort. As a result, violence accompanies alienation and fear on an everyday basis.[14] I think Peters is right about that and that the urban realities of alienation, fear, and violence make genuine relationship difficult.

This is why the concept of "covenant" is so important for urban ministry, for it represents a divine pattern for relationships that stands in marked contrast to prevailing modes of interrelation. In fact, the dominant symbol for most modern relationships is the "contract." A contract is based in negotiation and prescribes conditional relations with the other—"you do this, and I'll do that." In a relational contract, the meeting of stipulations is the only basis for continuing the relationship. In a related vein, sociologist Scott Greer describes the urban community as a "community of limited liability," because "the individual's investment is relatively small in the interactional network that constitutes the local group, and if his losses are too great he can cut them by getting out—the community cannot hold him. . . . [E]ven the most deeply involved can withdraw from the local community and satisfy all needs elsewhere."[15] The notion of "communities of limited liability" is one that urban churches need to ponder—perhaps especially predominantly white churches, which may be located in urban neighborhoods in which many of their members do not live and to which they would have tenuous commitments at best.

Consider the striking contrast between a "contract" and "community of limited liability" on the one hand and the symbol of a "covenant" on the other—a cruciform one at that. God's covenant with exiled Israel, described in Isaiah 61, is everlasting and unconditional. The demands of the covenant are right relations with God and others, and those "others" to whom we have genuine obligation include the most vulnerable: the oppressed, the broken-hearted, the captive, and the prisoner. In short, as the Great Commandment bears witness, living in covenant relationship with God entails both love of God and love of neighbor—even, and perhaps especially, the "crucified" neighbor—and never giving up on those whom God loves. Indeed, the very purpose of the urban church and its ministry is to increase love of God and the "vulnerable" neighbor."[16]

In summary, for all of these reasons, the symbol of the "cruciform cove-nant" is a powerful and evocative one for the practice of urban ministry. *Urban congregations and Christians are called to stand in covenant relation with God and others at intersections where God is bringing justice, reconciliation, and life out of the crucifixions that litter our landscapes.* Perhaps one further point needs to be made: such a covenant summons us to relationships with oth-ers—including vulnerable others—not out of charity or patronage, but because we recognize our own vulnerability in that of others, our own fear in theirs, our common experience of alienation, and the violence in us all. In recogniz-ing another's crucifixion, we discern our own—and these are the intersections where God is bringing life, because the truth of our faith is that our perceived strengths turn out to be weaknesses, and our weaknesses are the very place where God is bringing strength in and binding us together in covenant com-munity. Indeed, the central paradox of urban ministry is that justice, reconcili-ation, and sharing gifts emerge from the broken places in all our lives.

The Great Commandment

You will find that I also have a good bit to say about the Great Command-ment in connection with the cross, for it is through the lens of the cross that the heart is changed, enlarged, and redirected from crude self-interest toward God. In other words, it is through the power of the cross that, by God's grace, we are enabled to live into the dual love entailed by the Great Command-ment—love of God and of neighbor as self. I would contend that the very purpose of the urban church and its ministry is realized as it lives ever more fully into this commandment. So one last word on the Great Commandment, because it surfaces repeatedly throughout the discussion that follows.

In the Gospel of Mark, a scribe asks this question of Jesus: "Which com-mandment is the first of all?" And Jesus answers: "The first is, 'Hear, O

Israel: the Lord our God, the Lord is one; you shall love the Lord your God with all your heart, and with all your soul, and with all your mind, and with all your strength.' The second is this, 'You shall love your neighbor as yourself.' There is no other commandment greater than these." (Mark 12:28–31)

Heart, soul, mind, and strength—very few commentators have much to say about the varied elements of the self that are listed in the first commandment, tending to view them as distinctive aspects of the whole self. In short, the commandment enjoins us to love God with all of who we are.

However, I have found it intriguing and evocative to meditate on these different dimensions of the self as a means by which to grow more fully into the wholeness to which God calls us. Indeed, I've come up with an image for the Christian life that you'll hear more about later—that of a three-legged stool—that has been quite helpful to me as a means by which to facilitate conversation on integration (wholeness) in our practice of discipleship and ministry. As I imagine it, one leg of the stool is solidly grounded in the life of the mind[17] (as it is exercised and sharpened by theological and ethical reflection, biblical study, and careful attention to current events); a second leg is grounded in the power or strength of the will[18] (as it is manifest in social activism, for example—the active life of faith in both the church and the world); and a third leg is grounded in the contemplative life of the heart[19] (as it engages in communal worship and the practice of spiritual disciplines). The three legs of the stool are stabilized by a post or ring in the middle, representing the integration[20] of heart, mind, and will in our love of, and service to, God and neighbor. This three-legged stool is a model for ministry that I will use to evoke Jesus' summary of torah. Thus, I argue that the purpose of the urban church and its ministry is to integrate each leg of the stool in the whole of its ministry. In this way, the life of activism is never separate from the life of the mind; nor is the life of the heart, as it grows in love of the sovereign God of all creation, ever separate from growth in love of neighbor as self. Such integration stabilizes and strengthens our lives of faith, grounding and sustaining us amid the weighty challenges of urban ministry.

A Road Map

Here is a road map for the discussion ahead so that you can anticipate what is on the horizon. In chapter 1 we will consider this question: What does an inner-city grocery store have to do with the church? This question will prompt reflection on the relationship between the church and the world—one of the most basic questions for an urban church, with both practical and theological dimensions. Practically, it will engage the reality of food deserts in inner-city neighborhoods. Theologically, it will require reflection on our covenant life before the sovereign and cruciform God of all creation, whose will is abundance of life (including food) for all, not just the few. Four prepositions will help us engage these matters as we consider the church's calling to be *in, with, against,* and *for* the world.

Chapter 2 will explore a basic means by which a congregation can grow more fully into its identity as a covenant community. Urban churches can be very busy places, preoccupied with challenging tasks and activities. Focused and intentional relationship building is needed to counterbalance these preoccupations. I will introduce a community organizing tool—the one-on-one relational meeting—as a resource for creating covenantal community, because I believe that the relational meeting can be an invaluable aid for nurturing community and growth in love of God, neighbor, and self.

Chapter 3 will consider the foundational significance of the Great Commandment for the life of an urban church—a commandment that calls for the integration of heart, mind, and will as we embody love of God and neighbor, and thus has as its goal the wholeness or integrity of our lives of faith. Engaging the whole self in ministry is not easy, but it is not a solo venture. Indeed, it requires integration also into the life and ministry of a Christian community. In this chapter, another organizing tool, "the listening campaign," will be introduced that builds upon the one-on-one relational meetings of the previous chapter by broadening the conversation, engaging the whole community in collective discernment of the movement of God in its midst and directions in which it is being summoned as it seeks corporate embodiment of love of God and neighbor. Communal listening facilitates collective discernment and is a means by which we can integrate and engage our people in shared ministry.

Chapter 4 will address the contemplative as an indispensable aspect of deepening personal and corporate religious life as we engage in urban ministry. The contemplative entails both personal and corporate prayer and worship and creates the space in which we discover our yearning for God and God's yearning for us. The contemplative is also a milieu in which passion for justice and love of neighbor as self is nurtured. In this chapter, I will describe a project underway in the congregation I serve by which we are endeavoring to address the persistent need to bring the life of the heart into balance with the life of the mind and will as we grapple with the exacting challenges of urban life and ministry.

In sum, the first four chapters examine basic tools or practices that help us live into the Great Commandment in our practice of urban ministry. Engagement with them, however, evokes several questions in need of further attention. Thus, in chapter 5, I highlight four such questions that have occasioned significant teaching moments in the lives of the congregations I have served. The first is the question of Christ and culture, often prompted when the church employs tools and resources from other arenas of cultural endeavor (such as community organizing, the best management practices of the business community, or therapeutic wisdom). Are they fair game for use in the church, and how might theological reflection inform our deployment of them? The second question concerns the notion of "self-interest," a central concept in community organizing, as in politics, for it is assumed that one organizes around people's self-interest. Yet what does it mean for Christians to speak of "self-interest" when our model for Christian living is the self-giving love of God in Christ? I will articulate a Christian understanding of self-interest that I hope will address concerns about this matter. These two questions and the teaching moments they have occasioned have evoked other questions regarding Christian tradition and religious pluralism. If Christian faith is not insular to the life of the church but has significant ramifications for our life in the world, what do traditional beliefs, such as those expressed in the Apostles' Creed, have to do with urban life and ministry? And what does Christian witness look like in urban settings like Washington, D.C., where devotees of all the religions of the world reside? These last two questions, regarding tradition and religious pluralism, are crucial ones for the life and ministry of urban churches.

Chapter 6 will address one of the most critically divisive issues in urban America: race and poverty. This chapter reflects the experience of living in one of the most racially divided cities in the United States: Washington, D.C. It is an open wound in most major urban areas that many acknowledge but few address. I will describe a project launched by four neighboring churches in D.C., two largely white and two largely black, who engaged in covenant partnership to address directly the issue of racism and poverty in their community. This chapter will relate what happened and provide food for thought for congregational engagement with these crucial matters.

Chapter 7 will focus on jobs and living wages as a crucial concern in the life of urban communities and contend that advocating on their behalf is a worthy ministry for an urban church to engage. I have focused on jobs because work is an anchor for people's lives and because good work is good for all, just as bad work is detrimental for all and erodes the common good. I will argue that good work and fair wages are, for Christians, signs of resurrection—of God's overcoming of the crucifying effects of unjust labor on us all.

I hope the reflections in all of these chapters will provide food for thought for clergy and laypersons alike—indeed, for any who love both the city and the church and are engaged in urban ministry. I also hope it will be of use to those preparing for ministry, serving as a primer on basic considerations and practices vital to the life of urban congregations. Indeed, I hope it will encourage seminarians to consider a vocation in urban ministry as a worthy, challenging, and fulfilling calling. Each chapter concludes with either a "practicum" or "questions for further reflection" that I hope will facilitate deliberation on matters addressed and practical handles for grappling with them. All of the material in this book emerges from my personal experience and theological reflection in the trenches of urban ministry, in the company of congregations who have called me to join them in service to God and neighbor. I owe a special debt of gratitude to these good people, saints who embody a cruciform covenant, with whom it is my daily privilege to practice the Christian life.

Chapter 1

The Story of a Grocery Store

When the Super Fresh Grocery store in the Bolton Hill Shopping Mall of mid-city Baltimore, Maryland, closed in 2001, for some it was a "ho-hum" affair. Frankly, I found myself thinking, "good riddance." It was a bad store that seemed to have given up on the neighborhood a long time ago. The produce and meats it offered were mangy at best, and there was little variety. I'll never forget going to that store one morning before the early service at Brown Memorial Presbyterian Church to get bread for communion, and I couldn't find a decent loaf. It was a lousy store! But then, several months after the store closed, six of us from area churches that were a part of the BUILD organization (Baltimoreans United in Leadership Development, the local affiliate of the Industrial Areas Foundation) were invited to meet with residents of the neighborhood who had patronized the store.[1] People in the neighborhood agreed that the Super Fresh store was not what it should have been, and some were even angry about the quality of its merchandise. At the same time, all agreed on one point: it was their store. It was within walking distance, and they knew the people who worked there and most of the patrons. It was their store, even if it was a lousy store. It was a place where they could get produce and meat of some sort, even if it was not very fresh. We also learned that the store's closing meant significant hardship for neighborhood residents, most of whom did not have cars. The absence of a local grocery store within walking distance left them with two alternatives: they could travel to grocery stores at some distance on a city bus (using two different bus routes) or they could hire a "hack" (that is, an unofficial taxi that charged less than a licensed taxi to take them to the store). Either way they were caught in a bind. If they took the bus, there were limitations as to how much they could carry and any frozen goods were sure to thaw; if they took a hack, they could bring home a couple of weeks' worth of groceries but had to add an additional $15–$20 dollars to the cost because the hack had to wait while they shopped.

In recent years, what these residents were experiencing has been given a name: they were living in a "food desert," because they had to travel long distances to purchase fresh fruits and produce. In the Washington, D.C., area where I currently reside, "food deserts" coincide with income levels and are found only in poor districts of the city. Neighborhoods with the highest household income levels have the most grocery stores, including high-end stores such as Whole Foods. Correspondingly, neighborhoods with the lowest income levels have the lowest number of grocery stores, as well as the highest levels of obesity, because food is so often purchased at corner convenience stores where nutritious food is in short supply.[2] The Executive Summary of *When Healthy Food Is Out of Reach: An Analysis of the Grocery Gap in the District of Columbia — 2010* reports:

> In numerous cities across the United States, studies have documented a troubling "grocery gap": low-income and minority communities often have far less access to full-service grocery stores than do higher-income communities. Nationally, the grocery gap forces many low-income people to spend money and time traveling long distances to access food at full-service grocery stores. In some neighborhoods where full-service stores are absent, shoppers may rely on small corner or convenience stores, which often do not have sufficient healthy food and may charge higher prices for the limited nutritious food available.[3]

This account of life in Washington, D.C., in 2010 parallels what was happening in most inner-city neighborhoods of Baltimore during the twelve-year period from 1990–2002 when I was engaged there in ministry.[4] Until the Super Fresh Grocery Store closing in 2001, I had had little experience of Baltimore's "food gap," that is, the gap between poor and affluent neighborhoods in their access to healthful food.

Lettuce and God

The experience of listening to the stories of the Baltimore residents who had lost their grocery store raised an important theological question for me: What does a fresh, leafy head of lettuce have to do with the church? It is a question about the church's relationship to the world, or our covenant life before the sovereign and cruciform God of all creation. Of course, some argue that the church and the world are separate realms—that the church ought to focus on spirituality and stay out of the business of the world. In other words, the church ought to stay out of the lettuce business. Yet the centerpiece of my theological heritage is the notion of covenant life before the sovereign God of all creation, and God's sovereignty surely includes lettuce.

Thus I contend that the very heart of Christian theology—the doctrine of the sovereignty of God, as well as our covenant life in relationship with such a God—compels our engagement with questions of access to the basic gifts God has provided to nourish and sustain all life—gifts as basic as fresh lettuce or a decent loaf of bread. Why is it that some residents of our cities do not have access to such gifts? The reasons are racism and classism, which result in subpar living conditions in inner-city neighborhoods and in grocery stores that sell goods imported from the suburbs when their expiration dates have come and gone. Indeed, Gayraud Wilmore draws a direct connection between the doctrine of the sovereignty of God and opposition to the crucifying effects of racial prejudice when he observes, "The only sovereignty we acknowledge is God's. As Black and Reformed Christians we refuse to submit, as we did in slavery, to the control of any majority that arrogates to itself power that belongs only to God, especially power based on the assumption of racial superiority."[5]

H. Richard Niebuhr called attention to two very important implications of the sovereignty of God worth noting in this connection. He contended that first of all, if God is sovereign, we are called to a consistent *secularization* of all things, which means that there is no one sacred race, ethnicity, nation, religion, or place, because God alone is Lord of life and worthy of our ultimate devotion. Niebuhr contended that if God is sovereign, we are also called to *sanctify* all things, for in their appropriate relation to God, all things are beloved in God's sight. As Niebuhr put it, there are two great mottos that need to be kept before us: "I am the Lord thy God; thou shalt have no other gods before me" and "Whatever is, is good."[6] When our faith in the sovereign God is insufficiently secularizing on the one hand, or insufficiently sanctifying on the other, we run the risk of arrogating sovereignty to ourselves by bestowing God's special blessing on some people or places but not on others. And when this happens, there is almost always an abuse of power against someone or some portion of God's good creation. What does this have to do with our grocery store dilemma? It seems to me that if the executives of the Super Fresh grocery store were aware of the fact that closure of the store would create a "food desert" (and residents, with the help of their elected officials, ensured that they were aware of this consequence), then the decision to close the grocery store in the Bolton Hill Shopping Mall was tantamount to breaking the first commandment by arbitrating who gets to partake of God's good creation and who does not. When decisions like this are made, someone gets crucified! And the people in the neighborhood adjacent to my church were being crucified—exiled to a food desert! Decisions akin to the

closing of this grocery store are made all the time. Indeed, history is replete
with arrogations of divinity.

Tragically, all such arrogations of divinity are informed by what Walter
Brueggemann has described as the human myth of scarcity rather than by
God's litany of abundance. Indeed, he says the biblical history consists of a
struggle between the two. The opening chapters of Genesis tells the story of
a divine generosity and abundance so plentiful that no one can claim scarcity. But by the end of Genesis, Pharaoh appears on the scene and introduces
the principle of dearth. Pharaoh is fearful that there is not enough and starts
grabbing everything.[7] In fact, Pharaoh becomes the paradigm example of the
arrogation of divinity in the Bible.

In the Gospel of John, Jesus also consistently points to the abundance of
life and the goods of the earth when confronted with perceptions of scarcity.
The inaugural event of his public ministry counters scarcity with abundance,
when the wine runs out at a wedding in Cana (John 2:1–12). He averts a social
crisis by turning water into an extravagant amount of choice wine. Jesus'
goes on to describe the gift he represents by drawing on life-giving images,
claiming to be "the living water," "the bread of life" and the vine that sus-
tains many fruit-bearing branches (John 4:10, 15:1). When people experience
scarcity of life itself, as in the story of the death of Lazarus, Jesus announces,
"I am the resurrection and the life. Those who believe in me, even though
they die, will live, and everyone who lives and believes in me will never die"
(John 11:25–26). With declarations such as these, Jesus reverences life and
the goods of life in the face of human perceptions of scarcity. His images are
drawn from the ordinary stuff of this earth, the fabric of daily life. In other
words, he affirms one of the chief affirmations of Genesis 1: "whatever is,
is good." The abundance of life and the goods of life are not the exclusive
possession of any one group; they are to be shared. However, John's Gospel
conveys that people are both attracted to and repulsed by Jesus and his proclamation of abundance. And those repulsed by Jesus eventually crucify him.

We, too, crucify others whenever we claim exclusive privilege and hoard
the goods of the earth as our own or tolerate the fact that others do so. And
because crucifying patterns of scarcity amid abundance pervade our world,
I contend that God's sovereign trajectory in the world is best understood as
cruciform, for God is at work at such broken places, striving to bring life out
of death and abundance out of scarcity. Therefore, the interpretive lens by
which we are called to view the world is twofold and includes both suspicion
and grace. The lens of suspicion[8] asks the question, Who or what is being
crucified? The lens of grace asks the question, Where is God bringing life, or
resurrection and sanctification, out of the death-tending ways of the world?

A fully sovereign understanding of the cruciform God compels our engagement with a world in which God is already at work, bringing life out of our diminution.

The Church and the World

As I pondered the grocery store dilemma, it became clear to me that the task of the church and its ministry is to stand in covenant relation with God and others at points where the crucifying effects of the myth of scarcity are manifest, proclaiming God's litany of abundance. Douglas Ottati provides a helpful theological framework for this task. Ottati offers a description of the church's relation to the world using four prepositions: the church is *in, with, against,* and *for* the world.[9] I invite you to think about the church and the world, or our covenant life before the sovereign Trinitarian and cruciform God of all creation, using these prepositions. What does it mean for the church to be in, with, against, and for world? In short, what does lettuce have to do with the church?

"In" the World

Ottati's first descriptive preposition for the church's relation to the world is that the church is *in* the world, because the world is God's good creation. As Ottati puts it,

> The church is sent to all people and nations, and, therefore, is intentionally mixed into the world. It refuses to give up on what the faithful God refused to give up on. It honors the dynamic, intention, and pattern of the Word incarnate. . . . All of which says that this world, God's world, is neither alien nor strange for the church, but is partner, companion, and neighbor. Indeed, we can speak of solidarity of the church with the world, a solidarity that consists in the recognition that, since Jesus Christ is God's transformative way with the world, the church too should be in the world.[10]

One of the chief polarities recognized by organizations such as BUILD, founded on the principles of the Industrial Areas Foundation (IAF), is the tension between "the world as it is" and "the world as it should be." In "the world as it is," self-interest is the prime motivator for survival and leads to individualism and selfish behavior. The IAF, however, teaches that self-interest can actually be a relation-building, world-affirming motivation—it can move us toward the "world as it should be." The root etymology of the word "interest" is a combination of two Latin terms: *inter*, which can be translated "between" or "among," and *esse*, which can be translated "to be." Therefore, self-interest can mean something like "self interrelated to one's essence." What this suggests is that our interest is not trapped inside us but also resides within our relations with others.[11] Another way of putting the matter is that our essential selves are found in covenant relations to others and God.[12]

Some may question any notion of "self-interest" as a basis for relating to God and others. However, as Sondra Wheeler helpfully observes, "the ultimate moral ideal to which theologians like Augustine point is not really the suppression of self-love in favor of love for others. It is instead a vision of love rightly ordered, with the love of God being both the source and limit of all proper loves for created things. Only those who love God above all else can love God's creatures, including themselves, as they should."[13] Self-interest thus has everything to do with being in the world in relation to others and to God; it has everything to do with our covenant life before the sovereign God of creation. So when the BUILD churches in Baltimore entered into relationship with the residents who lived around that closed grocery store, it was not out of charity or even liberal activism. We got involved because it was essential to our being, for to live fully and abundantly is to live with and for others and with God, or to put it another way, to live a full covenant life before the sovereign God of creation.

As I reflected on such matters, I could not help but meditate on the fact that one of the best grocery stores in Baltimore, Fresh Fields (now Whole Foods), was in my own neighborhood. The store was elitist, it was expensive, and I couldn't always find what I needed there—indeed, I didn't know what to do with many of the gourmet items they sold. When I lived in Baltimore, I did not like going to Fresh Fields because I always felt underdressed, like something the "cat dragged in," compared to its fashionable patrons. Yet its produce was arguably the best in town. I once ate an extraordinary nectarine purchased at Fresh Fields that I remember to this day. It was so good and juicy and fresh that it easily would have been worth the short walk down the long hill from my house. Yet if I understand the doctrine of the sovereignty of God and covenant life before God correctly, that nectarine was not mine because I could afford it or because I lived close to a store that had fresh, luscious produce; it was first and foremost a gift from God's bountiful creation. As Psalm 24:1 affirms, "The earth is the LORD's and all that is in it, the world, and those who live in it." If being *in* God's good creation means that our essential being is found in relation to God and to others and in refusing to give up on what God refuses to give up on, then the church ought never to give up on the fullness of God's good gifts for all of God's children.

"With" the World

Many people do not experience the abundance of God's creation, and the church is complicit in this state of affairs. Thus, at the same time that we are *in* the world, we are also called to acknowledge that we are *with* the world, confessing our common faults and sins. During a follow-up meeting with the neighborhood residents, an elderly black woman asked, "It's been almost six months since that grocery store closed. Where have the churches been? Why haven't you done something about our grocery store?" I could have echoed the response of the one who was leading that meeting who said, "Well, we're here now." Or I could have stood up and offered a lofty and impassioned defense of the churches in this neighborhood, providing a litany of all the ministries in which we were engaged. But I had to confess that as the pastor of a pre-dominantly white urban parish, I had been blind to the plight of people in this neighborhood. They were, heretofore, invisible to me. To be sure, I had been involved in community organizing in Baltimore for several years. I was one of the leaders of BUILD when we organized Baltimore workers to help secure the first "living wage" bill in the country. But I didn't know all the practical realities of what life was like in the poor, predominantly black neighborhoods surrounding my church. I was captive to what Ottati calls "alien pieties that bring with them a train of myopic visions and practices . . . unresponsive to God and God's all-inclusive commonwealth."[14] And so when there was an opportunity to respond to the woman's question, I decided to remain silent and simply listen to the gospel spoken by someone who had been invisible to me. It was, in other words, a time for confession and penance.

"Against" the World

Confession, of course, is accompanied by a change in vision. It moves us to see the world in a different manner, in light of the sovereign God whose trajectory in the world is cruciform. The lens of suspicion prompts us to ask the question, Who is being crucified? And this question brings us to our next preposition. If the church is called to realize its essential life and purpose by being *in* the world of God's good creation where fresh, leafy lettuce and nectarines are meant for all, but is *with* the world that constricts our vision of who, in fact, has access to such produce, then the church is also simultane-ously *against* the world—which is to say that we are called to a prophetic witness, to stand with the disenfranchised. Ottati puts it this way:

Genuinely reforming churches will not shrink from the prophetic task.
. . . [T]hey will denounce the persistent scourges of racism, sexism, and
homophobia. They will point to severe economic disparities among communities linked in a single garment of global interdependence . . . . [The]
world may respond with benign neglect and refuse to take the church seriously. . . . In that case, prophetic churches have all the more reason to
remain in the world, refusing to leave it alone. [The church] has every
reason to be pests and persistent nuisances, calling into question business
as usual. . . . The prophetic task may have its cost and burdens. . . . The
task of faithfully objecting to the forfeiture of the good and abundant life
for which we are fitted may place the church into direct opposition to the
principalities, powers, and climates of opinion. . . . It may lead others to
question the church's good sense or prudence. . . . By the faithful logic
of theocentric devotion, none of these possibilities constitutes a reason to
relinquish or attenuate the critical and prophetic attitude. . . . God alone is
God, and we should serve no others. Reforming churches have to remain
true to the first commandment.[15]

The confession and subsequent vision given by the cruciform trajectory of
God made it clear to us that it was essential for the BUILD churches to stand
with the people in our neighborhood who had lost their grocery store. And
so our congregations began to organize meeting after meeting with folk who
lived in the inner-city neighborhoods surrounding the more affluent, gentrified
neighborhood of Bolton Hill. Soon multiple expressions of self-interest began
to merge. As people began to learn each other's faces and names, and most
important, their deepest yearnings for the neighborhood, it became clear that
everyone wanted a decent grocery store. Soon "us" and "them" became "we."

Two grocery store chains emerged as bidders for the contract to build a
store in the vacated site in the Bolton Hill Shopping Mall, and they agreed to
meet with our newly formed community. As usual with IAF-based organizations, before the meeting we made our demands known to representatives
of both grocery stores. These demands included fresh produce and meats
and accountability through periodic "surprise" inspections of the store. And,
as usual, they ignored the demands. Indeed, they came to the meeting fully
intending to "instruct" us on the grocery store business. But one of the feisty
leaders of the meeting, who was trained in IAF principles, would have none
of it. He pointed to the large blackboard on which our demands were listed
and informed the grocery store representatives that they each had ten minutes to respond to these demands. The first representative got up and said, "It
feels like you don't trust us very much." One of our neighborhood leaders
responded, "I've lived in this neighborhood for twenty years, and for twenty

years the grocery store in that shopping mall has been bad, so trust is earned!" Jeremiah might have been more poetic, but not more prophetic. It was summertime and there was sweltering heat in the fellowship hall of the Trinity Baptist Church that night, but our newly formed community provided the real heat. Both grocery store franchises reluctantly agreed to our demands. We ended the meeting by holding hands and praying for the future of our neighborhood. I guess you could say that we had already begun to interpret the world through the lens of grace, because life in that neighborhood certainly seemed more sanctified from that day forward.

Soon thereafter, I left Baltimore to become the pastor of The New York Avenue Presbyterian Church in Washington, D.C., but I heard reports about the new grocery store and its relationship with its neighbors. The store that was built in the Bolton Hill Shopping Mall was Stop Shop Save. After it opened, there were improved measures of accountability from the store toward the community. However, there were also complaints about the quality of the produce and the service provided—and these complaints are themselves a good sign that the neighborhood is holding the store accountable. Organizing is always reorganizing, so I hope and pray that the struggle goes on and the store and the people it serves continue to interact to everyone's benefit.

The use of power in IAF organizations deserves some comment in connection with this story. The power of organized communities is necessary for instituting change. Reinhold Niebuhr once suggested that the twin dangers in political community are anarchy and tyranny. Thus, power is necessary to avoid both extremes. As Langdon Gilkey observed of Niebuhr's thought, "No dominant group voluntarily surrenders its power and thus its privileges. . . . [R]ational and moral persuasion, while important, are not capable of dislodging a ruling group from its dominant position." He goes on to say that "The task of political life is not to achieve victory of one ideology or of one center of power over another, but to balance the forces within a community so that, on the one hand, a relative justice and peace are possible and that, on the other, the dangers of tyranny and anarchy are avoided."[16] While a grocery store chain may not seem like a "dominant group," when pitted against a community of poor black inner-city residents, they certainly hold the dominant power.

"For" the World

This brings us to the last preposition. If the church is *in* the world, never giving up on God's good creation, *with* the world, confessing our common faults and sins, and *against* the world, for the sake of the crucified and resurrected creation, then the church is also *for* the world because it is "a community of hope, which believes that if sin means derangement, then grace mean rearrangement. If sin means inordinate constriction, then grace means enlargement."[17] The passionate witness of the church is always to new possibilities. The biblical vision that guides us is that of a new heaven and a new earth (Rev. 21:22). Indeed, because God so loved the world and became incarnate among us, we have no other or higher calling than to stand in, with, and for our neighbors—in Baltimore, and beyond—so that the grocery store just a few blocks from my former church might someday be filled with the best lettuce and nectarines and cantaloupes and fresh corn that God's good earth can offer. Our calling is to proclaim God's will for us in Christ, that all might have life, and have it abundantly (John 10:10). Ottati's eloquent words about reforming faith provide an appropriate conclusion to these reflections and inspiration for the ministries before us:

> Within the frame of reforming piety, then, this is what it means to say that the God disclosed in the histories of Israel and of Jesus Christ is sovereign. The arc of the universe is God's arc, and this arc, although we cannot always make out its curvature, bends toward God's universal commonwealth, kingdom, or city. Finally, not without confessing sins, not apart from judgments, prophetic criticisms, chastening defeats, and passionate sufferings, reforming piety supports a truly cosmic optimism. The God of grace and glory, the power of goodness made perfect in weakness, is greater than the power of evil. . . . This is why the church is *for* the world.[18]

May God grant us wisdom and courage for this vocation!

Practicum

Now I invite you to apply these reflections in your own ministry context. I will provide a very brief description of community organizing basics. Then following this short overview, I will suggest ways in which you might begin to think about acts of ministry to which God may be calling you in your community.

Let me first review some of the basic practices of community organizing. Mike Gecan speaks of four tools for effective organizing and analyzing of one's congregation and community. These tools are (1) the individual (relational) meeting; (2) power analysis of both the church and the institutions in the community; (3) teaching and training; and (4) action and evaluation.[19] Since I devote chapter 2 of this book to the individual meeting, I will speak only briefly here about this important organizing tool. The individual meeting is not a friendly chat but rather a focused conversation about passions and self-interests that can help two people begin to reflect together on the world as it is and the world as it should be. It can move people from insularity toward shared concern and partnership. In this chapter, I have described how *relational meetings* helped us learn what a grocery store meant to the community around us. Relational meetings should be conducted within one's own church (see chapter 2 on this point) and in one's community. For now, let me focus for a moment on the latter: Consider the institutions in the neighborhood of your congregation, be they mom-and-pop fast-food stores, restaurants, retail stores, residences, homeless shelters, and, of course, the institutions of city government in your locale. You could invite the owners or workers in these institutions, folk who live in the community (who are not part of your congregation), homeless folk, or your city council member, to sit down for one-on-one conversations about their lives and the community (a more detailed description of the nature of these conversations will come in the following chapter). Among other things, you are listening for stories of the issues they face (e.g., safety issues, affordable housing, poverty, etc.). You can't address all of the world's problems in relational meetings, but you might find common ground for action. And you may discover potential leaders in your community who can galvanize common action.

A *power analysis* of both church and community begins with the relational meeting, because in these meetings you discover the leaders of your community. Power analysis also gets at issues like poverty and wealth in a community (and the city). It tries to construct a map of the power relations in a locale, exploring the whys and wherefores of this power: Who has it and how did they get it? How do they hold it? And how do they share it (or fail to do so)? If homelessness is an issue in your community, why is this the case? Are living wage jobs available? (Many homeless people work, but the wages they earn do not enable them to afford housing). It is important that your congregation reflects on the power dynamics in your community.

Teaching and training leaders is key to congregational action. Most people in your congregation have some vision for the "world as it should be," some clarity about the "world as it is," and maybe even some sense for how to move from one to the other, but they are seldom challenged to do so. I invite you to teach and train in a manner that creates a relational culture that allows for positive tensions and accountability. There is such a thing as "good tension"—the tension that moves people to act on a common problem, like the sometimes tense interactions between the executives of the new grocery story and the store's customers. Yet most people avoid tension like the plague, so I encourage you to address the constructive role of "good tension" in the life of a community.

Then, *action and evaluation*: a congregation needs to act and then evaluate the action. The action does not have to be big. In fact, I encourage you to start with small actions: perhaps you could address a safety issue of common concern in your community or undertake a project to assist the homeless (e.g., a clothes closet). Then evaluate the action, considering questions like, How did the action change your congregation and the relationship of your congregation to your community? Remember, an action is as much about how it changes us as it is about how an issue is resolved. In the grocery store scenario, the real action was on our churches and the surrounding community and how we moved from "us" and "them" to "we."

Let me finally say a few words about articulating our faith in the public arena. I never shy away from expressing my faith in the public arena, but I try to do so in a way that seeks common ground with others who do not share my faith. So if it is your conviction, as it is mine, that God is sovereign over all of life and that we have covenant responsibilities before God and others, then it is critical that we articulate clearly the faith upon which we are acting. In so doing, I commend the four prepositions that I used in this chapter: the church is simultaneously *in, with, against,* and *for* the world. Thus, let me conclude this practicum by offering a series of questions to help you reflect on your own ministry setting.

The church is *in* the world because the world is God's good creation and the church should refuse "to give up on what the faithful God refused to give up on."[20] The assumption here is that God is already present, sustaining, redeeming, and liberating the world. Where do you see God's presence in your community? What institutions or persons are a sustaining presence in your community, and how might this presence be the face of God in your locale? Where do you see God's redeeming presence at work in your community? That is, are there institutions or people working for homecoming for those living in exile (e.g., think of services for the homeless or mentally ill)? Where do you see God's liberating presence in your neighborhood? That is, are there institutions or persons working to liberate people from oppression (e.g., battered women's shelters or counseling centers)? How might you partner with or support these institutions or people?

The church is also *with* the world, confessing common faults and sins. My basic assumption here is that, for Christians, the cross of Jesus exposes the crosses that litter the landscape of our world, as well as our own complicity (through sins of commission or omission) in them. Consider one example: with every economic downturn, city governments invariably cut programs that empower and assist the marginal. Is this happening in your neighborhood? And if so, what has anybody done about it? If the answer to this question is "nothing" or "not much," then confession and penance is warranted. There is a reason why Christian experience always begins with penance. Any serious prophetic impulse arises from a penitential foundation—a base that draws our attention to the crosses of our community as well as to our complicity in or toleration of them, and then this draws our vision toward the arc of God, bringing resurrection and life out of the crucifying patterns of our world. The prophetic impulse does not stem from liberal do-goodism, because the fact of the matter is that we are not all that good! The prophetic impulse stems from a penitential theology grounded in the sure reality of a merciful God in whom alone is our help and who forgives, restores, heals, and empowers us for the prophetic task of mending of creation.

If confession draws our attention to crosses that litter our landscape and to our sins of commission of omission that permit them, then it also compels us to stand *against* the world in prophetic witness and action. In this chapter, I have argued that we are called to stand at points where the crucifying effects of the myth of scarcity are manifest, proclaiming God's litany of abundance. Where and how can you stand with people and institutions in your community against the principalities and powers that directly or indirectly oppress others and create scarcity? To be sure, no one will admit to being the oppressor, but Reinhold Niebuhr wisely observed that the twin dangers of our common life are tyranny and anarchy: one leads to active oppression and the other to confusion and inactivity. So when a city government cuts poverty programs that affect people in your community, they must be called to account for it. Otherwise, tyranny and anarchy reign.

Finally, the church is called to be *for* the world. Indeed, we ought to be cosmic optimists about our community because the God who is sovereign in our locale is always about the work of bringing life out of death-tending behaviors. I invite you to a simple expression of thanksgiving for everything in your community that is hopeful and encourage you to express that thanksgiving actively. If someone is running a local shelter or soup kitchen, take that person to lunch to thank them for what they are doing. Or perhaps your church could sponsor a lunch or breakfast for its staff and volunteers. We don't do these kinds of things enough, but they are simple acts that can bind us in the covenant that we seek in our communities and to the God whose love, grace, and justice are for all people.

Chapter 2

Creating Covenant Community

The Relational Meeting

Philosopher Hannah Arendt once observed that "human essence . . . can come into being only when life departs, leaving nothing but a story."[1] At first glance, I assumed she was referring to what we learn about an individual after he or she has died, for death is the occasion for telling stories about the dearly departed. Whenever I am with the family of someone who has just passed away, before we do anything else—even before we plan the details of the memorial service—we often simply tell stories. Stories get to the essence of what the family feels about the one who has died. In fact, on such occasions, I often learn more about a person than I knew when he or she was alive, and I feel sad about this. I often leave such encounters with a sense of loss, not just because of the death itself, but also because I wish I had known some of these stories when that person was alive because they would have helped me connect with him or her more deeply. Stories help us understand what makes people tick, what animates their lives.

However, upon further reflection, I realized that there might be another way to understand Arendt's observation—poetically, rather than literally. Literally, her words might refer to death, but poetically they could also refer to life and to the way in which life issues from stories—stories about our relationships to one another and to God; stories about family, friends, vocation, mentors; stories of joy, pain, passion, anger, injustice, healing, liberation, and redemption. One of the reasons that Jesus is central to the life and faith of Christians is because of the stories that are told about him—about his life, ministry, death, and resurrection. They are stories that animate our own.

One of the most distinctive aspects of the story of Jesus, as the Gospel of Luke tells it, is the way Jesus eats. Indeed, it has been observed that Jesus is always eating in Luke. He is always going to, or coming from, a meal. We find the theme of eating much more in Luke than in any other Gospel, and clearly there is more going on at table than the ingesting of food. The sharing of food provides the occasion for deep relationship building. As an example, consider the story of the risen Lord's encounter with two disciples on the road to Emmaus in Luke 24, which can be seen as a case study in relationship building. En route to Emmaus, Jesus engages in conversation with two disciples who do not recognize him. He walks by their side, asks several pointed questions, and listens carefully to their story, which is one of grief over the crucifixion of one whom they had followed. He challenges them with the traditions of their faith recorded in Scripture (stories of Moses and the prophets) and then interprets his own life, death, and resurrection by weaving the story of Israel into his own. When they arrive at the village of Emmaus, the disciples invite him to join them at table, where he breaks bread with them, and at that moment their eyes are opened and they recognize the risen Christ in their midst. This story recounts a moment of deep relationship building that is at the core of Luke's Gospel. It is often recounted when we celebrate the Eucharist, or Lord's Supper, because the sacrament reenacts the story of Jesus, and in the breaking of bread, our eyes, too, are opened and we recognize the presence of the risen Christ in our midst. In other words, as we partake of the sacrament, Jesus' story becomes our story and the risen Christ animates our life together as a community of faith.

It is instructive to view community organizing through the lens of the story of Emmaus, for this story exemplifies the power of the relational meeting wherein animating stories are shared and embodied. The relational meeting is considered the primary tool for community organizing because it is the fundamental building block of any community or congregation. Ed Chambers claims that there are two ways of acting in the world: one is task oriented and the other is relational, and the latter is far more powerful for it can be the means for achieving many tasks. The relational meeting is the "glue" that enables people to embrace the tension between what community organizers refer to as the "world as it is" and the "world as it should be."[2] Louise Green offers a succinct description of what the relational meeting entails:

What is a 1-to-1 meeting?

- A 30–45 minute meeting for face-to-face conversation with one person
- Getting to know the other person and being known
- An inquiry into what matters to a person and why
- A chance to go outside of the repetitive tasks and small group activities that dominate congregational and organizational life
- An opportunity to know the private motivations each person has for doing public action such as congregational volunteerism or social justice work

- A search for leaders and participants with the talent, motivation, initiative, energy, or anger to change a situation
- A way to identify issues that need to be addressed and are not a part of the current action plan[3]

Such meetings hold enormous promise, because we seldom attend to the fundamental dimensions of relationships. In ancient cultures table fellowship was a prime time for relation building, but in our day we often eat on the run or in front of the TV. Moreover, while the "wired world" has connected us in wonderful ways never before imagined, it has also disconnected us in other respects. In our everyday lives, often overwhelmed with busyness and tasks, we seldom attend to the deeply relational stuff of life that creates binding connections with others. We live in a bureaucratic world where meetings, agendas, and tasks reign supreme. These things are, of course, important, but too often we lose sight of an overall vision of what God is calling us to be and do. The church was called into being to embody and engage a ministry of reconciliation for the purpose of building redemptive, liberating, and covenantal relationships; but even in church we can become so task-oriented that we easily lose sight of our calling.

The Relational Meeting Campaign

For all of the reasons noted above, in the spring of 2010, the session (the governing board) of The New York Avenue Presbyterian Church decided to set aside six to eight months to do relational meetings within the congregation. Fifteen people agreed to initiate as many as ten one-on-one meetings with parishioners, and the agenda for these meetings was to be nothing other than relationship building, the hearing and telling of stories, on the assumption that when we hear and tell stories that are meaningful to us and discern commonalities within our stories, something redemptive happens. We announced to the congregation that when someone called and asked for a relational meeting, they did not need to prepare for anything other than the giving of thirty to forty-five minutes of their time. All they needed to do was to show up ready to hear and to tell stories. The meetings could follow the biblical tradition of sharing a meal, the more modern tradition of conversation over coffee, or could simply involve sitting down in a quiet place and sharing.

As we might have expected, the good folk of NYAPC responded with the question, "Why? To what purpose? What is to be the end product of these relational meetings?" We tried to answer this question by underscoring the sheer revolutionary act of building relationships. We acknowledged that issues, dreams, and visions might, and hopefully would, emerge out of these relational meetings that we might later want to act on, but we did not want to move ahead too fast. *Our initial focus was on forging relationships— creating a covenantal culture of deep and binding connection.*

Another significant question emerged and had to be addressed: Are the tools of "community organizing" alien to the church and Christianity? It was a legitimate question. In fact, it was a question with which I, too, had found myself wrestling during my Industrial Areas Foundation training in 1990, and ever since. It is, in part, the impetus for this book. In response to this important question, I conducted teaching sessions with the boards of NYAPC on the difference between what H. Richard Niebuhr called "Christ of culture" and "Christ transforming culture."

While people may be attracted to Christianity because its teachings are in sync with the best of cultural teaching and philosophy,[4] Christ cannot simply be equated with the highest values of culture (Christ of culture). Culture is fallen and in need of transformation (Christ transforming culture). As Niebuhr puts it (describing the position of Christ transforming culture), "The problem with culture is therefore the problem of its conversion . . . though the conversion is so radical that it amounts to a kind of rebirth."[5] So the question for the Christian is not whether the worldly wisdom of community organizing is valuable; rather, the question is whether the tools of community organizing can be placed into conversation with the Christian story of sin and salvation in such a way that the former is transformed into cruciform, liberating practices for the Christian life.

Good conversation ensued, so much so that I promised to preach on the topic. I decided to do so on Easter Sunday morning. It was a risky decision, because Easter is, after all, an occasion on which marginal Christians are likely to make a rare appearance, and a sermon offering a theological perspective on the relational meeting might seem odd to some. But because it was and is my conviction that a Christian construal of the tools of community organizing gets to the heart of the Christian faith, I deemed the risk worth taking.

"ANIMATING STORIES"

Easter 2010

Isaiah 65:17–25
Luke 24:1–12

I'm increasingly persuaded that, for Christians, our core story, the story that animates our lives, follows the pattern of Easter—that of crucifixion and resurrection. For example, if I were to ask you to tell your animating story, what would it be? What is the story that goes to your core, your deepest passion—the story, in other words, that animates your life? Now without question, we may not have just one animating story, but rather multiple stories that evolve over time. But my suspicion is that all of our stories have something of the pattern of Easter to them—something about the emergence of life out of struggle, of redemption out of brokenness, of light out of darkness.

For instance, I recently had dinner with a minister colleague who has just moved into the area. His name is J. Herbert Nelson, and he is the new Director of the Office for Public Witness of the PCUSA, the office that is the public face of the Presbyterian Church on national and international issues about peace, poverty, and other social issues. We were just getting to know each other, exchanging "niceties"—stuff about our ministries and families and history—important information, but we were just scratching the surface. It occurred to me that we could go on and on like this through the entire meal and never get to know one another. So I asked him the question I just asked you: if you were to tell me your animating story, the story that goes to your core, what would it be? Without hesitation, he told me the story of growing up as a minister's kid in North Carolina. Every Christmas morning, before he could open his presents, his father would take him out to deliver Christmas presents to poor families in the area where they lived. But they did more than just deliver the presents. They would enter the homes of the people and sit and talk to them for a while before leaving. So his memories of Christmas morning were of sitting with his father in homes where you could look up and see holes in the ceilings or look down through holes in the floor and see the dirt underneath the house. This story told me more about him than if he had given me his résumé because it told me something about his core and how the risen Christ is present in his life, animating his ministry to alleviate poverty and injustice. In other words, J. Herbert's story follows the pattern of Easter—that of life emerging out of the death-tending ways of our world.

His story then prompted me tell one of my own. It is the story of a man named Ripley, or Rip, as he liked to be called. I met Rip in Baltimore when a group of us from BUILD (Baltimoreans United In Leadership Development) churches were trying to understand why working folk were showing up at our soup kitchens. Rip was a friendly man whom I met as he was filling out an application to do temporary work. He had kind eyes and an inviting smile. My guess was that he was in his late fifties or early sixties—not old enough for a social security check, but too old to be doing the kind of hard labor that was the only work he was able to find. He was hired daily to do jobs no one else wanted to do, usually very hard jobs like cleaning up construction sites. He told me that the most he had ever earned in his life was $6 an hour, and that every time he made enough money to live on, he got laid off. But he said he had never been on public subsides. He had always worked. He said he wanted to work. On Saturdays he went to the breakfast program at his local church because it saved on the food bill. Finally, I asked him the question that plagued me the most as I heard his story: "How do you keep going?" Rip smiled, looked skyward and said: "God helps me—God helps me!" I now find that I always think of Rip when I serve communion to our homeless folk in the Radcliffe Room [New York Avenue's Homeless Ministry] or when I encounter a worker cleaning a bathroom or the streets. My memory of him prompts me to remember that the risen Christ is present among "the least of these"—especially present among the working poor, the homeless, the discouraged. Rip's story helps me look to the God who raised Jesus from the dead and who calls me to imagine and work for the day spoken of in our morning text from Isaiah—the day when people will not only build houses, but also live in them.

Being a Christian is an exercise in memory—not just any memory, but animating memory. Animating stories, by definition, move us to act *"in the world as it is"* in order to move it toward *"the world as it should be."* Animating stories are personal and communal narrations of how the risen Christ is present in our midst.

Another of my animating stories is about the death of my father at age sixty-seven. I was only twenty-seven years old when he died, and it happened way too soon, before I felt I really got to know him. His death brought me face-to-face with the realization that life is fleeting, and that I spend way too much time on the surface of it. I regret that I never spent the kind of quality time with my father needed to learn his animating story. I now know that this was one of the motivating factors that led me to pursue ministry so that I might get to the core of how God is present in peoples' lives and how our stories follow the pattern of Easter—that is, how they move us from "the world as it is" to "the world as it should be." Animating stories are Easter stories. They are often stories about grief over the death of a loved one and how it brought us into deep relationships with others who are grieving. Sometimes they are stories of depression or traumatic experiences that eventually brought about transformation of our lives and circumstances, stories of how we found life therein.

Our morning Scripture reading from Luke is about animating stories—Easter stories. Grief stricken women, disciples of Jesus, came to the tomb to prepare the body of Jesus for burial, and much to their surprise they found that the stone sealing the tomb had been rolled away and the body of Jesus was nowhere in sight. Two messengers in dazzling white clothing then gave them, and us, all the information needed to evoke our own Easter stories. Their first key question was this: "Why do you look for the living among the dead?" Now the most obvious point of this question was to highlight the fact that Jesus had been raised from the dead—so why were they lingering around tombs? But there is certainly a more existential or spiritual point to this question. A moment's reflection will reveal how much of our time we spend on trivial pursuits—how much of our time we spend sleepwalking through life. And because of this we often don't get to the revolutionary core of our lives where the spirit of the living God is moving, challenging, confronting our complacency. We too often miss the deep questions—the Easter questions.

But to get to these questions we need one more vital piece of information, and so it is important that we hear the next statement that the messengers gave to the women on that first Easter morn as well: remember what he told you, that he would be crucified by sinners "and on the third day rise again." Core stories almost always follow the pattern of Christ in crucifixion and resurrection. Indeed, it is in such stories that the risen Christ is most present to us. They are often stories of pain or passion or even anger at the world as it is—a place that in one way, shape, or form crucifies us all. Yet a core story also animates new life and motivates us to move in that direction. Core stories, in other words, are about the experiences of discovering the surprise of resurrection, of discovering and being discovered by the same God who raised Jesus from the dead. These are the kinds of stories that are often told at table, during a meal. In Luke's Gospel, for example, it happens in just this manner. The first resurrection appearance came to two sad disciples who did not recognize the risen Christ in their very midst until they told stories and broke bread together. In fact, when you leave here today, I encourage you to read the Emmaus story in Luke 24—which immediately follows Luke's Easter story and is also the assigned text for our reflection this Easter evening. Then when you are breaking bread at table or drinking coffee together, invite a sharing of core or animating stories, the kind of stories wherein you might just recognize the risen Christ in your midst.

To spur you on, we will partake today of Communion, which is, after all, a model for all our eating. For at this table, we share bread and cup in remembrance of the core story of our faith. And as we do so, we trust on the promise that it will animate our own individual stories. The worst thing one can do is to eat unconsciously—that is, to eat without memory, without a consciousness of the food we eat or where it came from—or without real consciousness of the person or persons with whom we are eating and of their core, animating Easter stories. As a fast-food culture, we eat unconsciously all the time, and often alone. Unconscious eating can be the source of great injustice when we do not call to mind the faces and hands of the people who planted and harvested the food, who prepared and served it. Did they receive a decent wage for doing so? What injuries may they have suffered to provide the food before us? What risks did they have to take?

But when we repeat the words of institution for the Lord's Super, we do not eat unconsciously. We remember. We say, "This do in remembrance of me," and in so doing we are re-membered as the body of Christ, the one who was broken, tortured, executed, but whom God raised from the dead. Communion can become the animating story for our own stories. It can be an occasion for rediscovery of the Easter pattern in our own lives.

So back to the original question: What is your animating story? Or more to the point, where do you find your core story in the pattern of Easter's life-giving faith? As you think about this question hear again these words of Luke about the presence of the risen Christ at table with disciples who failed to recognize him and ponder how these words might be true for you: "When he was at the table with them, he took bread, blessed and broke it, and gave it to them. Then their eyes were opened, and they recognized him." And so also will the risen Christ be present for us.

Amen.

Easter sermons have always been a challenge for me because the range of people present for an Easter service makes it hard to identify your target audience. Do you address your sermon to the faithful who have traveled through the season of Lent and Holy Week, to the neglect of folk who barely know the Christian story? Do you target the people who rarely come to church in hopes of engaging them with the central message of the Christian faith? Or do you focus somewhere in between and risk missing both? In this sermon, I focused somewhere in between and the results were unclear to me. I have never done an exit interview with people leaving a worship service, but I would like to have done so after Easter services in 2010. I wish I could have interviewed some of them during lunch afterward and asked about their animating stories.

I can report one memorable response that I received right after the early service on that Easter Sunday. As I was standing in the narthex talking with visitors, a church member came up to me and blurted out, in a half-quizzical, half-exasperated tone, "Roger, I don't think I have an animating story!" At first I was dumbstruck and felt that my best efforts had failed to communicate. (They probably had!) But I knew him to be a person of great depth. He was in the State Department's diplomatic corps and had been serving with extraordinary dedication in troubled spots throughout the Middle East, supported by his young family who shared his commitment to diplomatic service and the challenging lifestyle it entailed. I also knew that his brother had died of cancer when he was a young boy—an experience that left an indelible mark upon him, for in the past, he had spoken to me with great passion about this experience. So I said to him, "Andrew, of course you've got an animating story! Let's set up a time to talk about this." And we did. I learned from that conversation that the very terms I had been using—like "core story" or "animating story"—needed further explanation. For Andrew, an invitation to talk about his "life calling" more clearly enabled him to identify and articulate the deep story of his life. And, to be sure, he had a deep story to tell.

As the weeks passed and as members of the congregation began to participate in relational meetings, other questions emerged. One that challenged me to think more deeply about animating stories was this: Does an animating story always follow the pattern of death and resurrection? Great question! If, in a relational meeting, I ask someone about his or her core stories, I might anticipate hearing about the birth of a child, a marriage, or a significant relationship. But a relational meeting also involves what community organizers call "agitation" or challenging people to go deep into their pain and anger about the brokenness in the world. This is exactly what Jesus did with two disciples on the road to Emmaus. So, for me, the question about whether or not an animating story has to follow the pattern of Easter—the pattern of death and resurrection—is like asking, Have I sinned, and do I live in a fallen world, and do I believe God has the power to redeem me?"

Dying and Rising

I am known for chasing rabbits and am inclined to chase one right now because I think this particular rabbit is relevant to this discussion of animating stories and Easter patterns of sin and salvation. I have always felt that one of my responsibilities as a minister, trained in the life of the mind, is to raise questions about pain, anger, and brokenness and then to bring substantive theological reflection to bear on engagement with them. I never shy away from bringing the foundational figures of my Reformed theological heritage to bear on such questions—people like John Calvin or the Niebuhr brothers—and I deeply appreciate theologians like Serene Jones who bring Calvin and other founding figures into conversation with feminist and liberation theology. Jones's retrieval of Calvin's perspective on sin and grace is particularly compelling, and I have referred to it many times in sermons and conversation with parishioners.

For example, I like Jones's retrieval of Calvin's description of sin as a self "despoiled" or stripped of one's skin (that is, of one's boundaries or integrity). Jones notes that the loss of boundaries can happen in many ways: "[W]hen sin wears the face of exploitation, the borders of the self are plundered by economic powers that extract women's labor for another's use. . . . When sin wears the face of powerlessness, the self is 'unsheathed' insofar as it is denied any control over its environment. . . . When sin wears the face of marginality, women . . . disappear from the register of social meaning."[6] Some of the members of my congregation seem to be getting at the same notion when they speak of "authenticity" or the lack thereof, because it is a loss of integrity and authenticity that many of them experience when they find themselves marginalized in our world because of global economic inequalities or discrimination due to gender or sexual orientation.

Moreover, Jones notes that we are responsible both for injustices done to us as well as those we do to others. Yet it is complicated, because she also recuperates Calvin's notion of sin as the "imprisoned will" to describe what it is like to be born into oppressive social practices from which one can never entirely escape. It is highly unlikely that we will ever fully extricate ourselves from systems of oppression, but knowing this points us toward the good that God intends for us all and thus never lets us rest or relieves us from the responsibility of living into God's empowerment of ourselves and others.[7]

In short, sin is multifaceted. The classic definition of sin as pride or as an overabundance of self must be expanded by the experience of others, for whom sin may entail denigration of self. And if sin is too little or too much self, then classic doctrines like justification (or the gift of right relation to God) and sanctification (or growth in grace) need revision. Jones provides an intriguing reappraisal of these doctrines. She suggests that they speak to two different aspects of the human condition. For some, God is working to convict us of sin or to deconstruct an overabundance of self and bring us into right relation with God and others—or justification. For others, especially women and marginalized people, the problem is not having enough self, and thus God is working to form an authentic self in Christ that can relate to God and others—or sanctification.[8]

I have chased this rabbit because it is vitally related to the question of whether or not animating stories follow the pattern of Easter—of death and resurrection—because it is my conviction that they do follow this pattern. To put this more precisely, my faith tells me that we are all stuck in patterns of too little or too much self in societies that perpetuate both schemes, and we are all desperately in need of deliverance and redemption. We need construction and deconstruction in personally appropriate doses. Thus in some way, shape, or form, it does seem to me that our core, animating stories will reflect something of this framework.

But I digress. You may be wondering how the relational meeting campaign went. Let me tell a few of the animating stories I learned. A woman shared her experience as part of the sanctuary church movement that emerged in the 1980s and 1990s to provide safe-haven for Central American refugees fleeing persecution. The stories she shared of these refugees were heartbreaking and horrific but inspired her to go to law school. She now heads a nonprofit organization providing legal assistance to immigrants. Moreover, given the harsh immigration laws in this country and the number of immigrant workers who show up to eat breakfast at our Radcliffe Room ministry to the homeless on Sunday mornings, she is interested in how the church might get more involved in this issue. I also learned the story of a middle-aged man, a deacon, who has emerged as one of the leaders in our homeless ministry. He spoke of the fire that has grown in his heart for work with the homeless, so much so that he yearned to do it full-time. He never used the word "authenticity" for this work, but I gathered that the word would capture something of what he was experiencing. A young adult woman spoke of her sister who has a cognitive disability. As her parents aged, they spoke to her about how, one day, she would have to take over the care for her sister. She did not speak of this as an onerous burden but rather as a familial calling. In each of these stories, I heard something of the Easter pattern of their faith or of how the Spirit of God is moving in their lives, deconstructing a world that made no room for immigrants, homeless folk, or people who have cognitive disabilities and constructing a grace-filled, life-giving world where people can be treated with dignity, be cared for, or be empowered to seek justice.

Others who did relational meetings heard similar stories to such a degree that it soon became clear to me that something of a cultural shift was taking place in the congregation: we were becoming a more covenantal community. When you know somebody's story, it changes the way you are in community with each other. If a cultural shift is taking place, it will need cultivation, because one thing I have learned about a relational (versus task-oriented) culture is that it takes time and intentionality. But we have made a start. James Madison once said, "Great things can only be accomplished in a narrow compass."[9] I think he is right about that. The next step was to bring even more people into the relational process and into the communal process of discerning how the Spirit of God was moving in our midst, shaping us for new directions in ministry. Thus, in the summer of 2010, we engaged in a listening campaign that will be described in the following chapter.

Practicum

As in chapter 1, I now invite you to apply these reflections in your own ministry context. The relational meeting can be a powerful, biblically-based, theologically-grounded tool to build covenant relationships within your congregation. The relational meeting can also help identify leaders in your community. In what follows, I will first describe how to do a relational meeting campaign, and then suggest how relational meetings might become part of the everyday lifeblood of your church.

Yet before getting to these practical discussions, let me summarize my assumptions about the relational meeting. The relational meeting is not an alien tool for the church if we bring these tools into transformational conversation with our faith. So I want to challenge the assumption that the relational meeting is simply a community organizing tool to build relationships and get things done in the church or community. Rightly understood, the relational meeting can be, for Christians, an experience of conversion, or what one might call a mini-Easter experience of dying and rising. Such a meeting can draw us out of insular worlds toward the essence of what God has called us to be and do, which entails increasing love of God, neighbor, and self. In his fine book on the relational meeting, *The Power of Relational Action* (one that I heartily recommend to you), Ed Chambers speaks of this meeting as the mixing of spirits.[10] I think this is right, but I would also add another perspective on the relational meeting. It is a microcosmic experience of what I spoke of earlier as the three-legged stool metaphor wherein the Spirit of God expands our constricted hearts, minds, and wills. H. Richard Niebuhr once said that in every dialogue there is a third (i.e., God) who is moving to break open closed circles, and this third "does not come to rest until the total community of being is involved."[11] So I trust you can see that the relational meeting is, for me, vitally important!

But how do you go about organizing a relational meeting in your church? Here are the nuts and bolts. First of all, I would urge your church leadership to learn more about the importance and potential of the relational meeting. They could read this chapter, Ed Chambers's short book on relational action, or both. I also commend to you Jeff Krehbiel's fine book, entitled *Reflecting with Scripture on Community Organizing*.[12] If there is an affiliate organization of the Industrial Areas Foundation in your area, I strongly recommend inviting one of their organizers to a special session to speak on the subject of the relational meeting. During this training I would emphasize the difference between a task-oriented meeting and a relational meeting.

I would then emphasize the distinction between private and public meetings. A private meeting is about friendships, family, and close relations. A relational meeting, however, is a public meeting about our common life together. It is about animating stories that give a sense for what makes people who they are and for the gifts, leadership qualities, and energies that they bring to the tasks of ministry. Public meetings are open and transparent and are about our life in the congregation and in the world. They are about commitments and accountability, dignity and respect in both congregation and world.[13] The private and public distinction is community organizing language and it is fine as far as it goes, but religious folk need a language that is more vigorous, life-giving, and transformative. In the first chapter, I explicated the heart of the Christian faith as covenant life before the sovereign cruciform God of all creation who refuses to give up on what God has created. For me, covenant language is the appropriate language for the public aspect of the relational meeting. This may sound strange to some religious people because we have grown so accustomed to thinking about religion as an exclusively private matter—and there is, to be sure, a private dimension to our relationship with God. But if God is truly sovereign and calls us to covenant life with both God and others, then our relationship to God is also profoundly public. So in teaching about the difference between private and public meetings, I urge you to use the covenant language of our faith, because any relational meeting worth its salt is not just a dialogue, but a trialogue—one in which God, too, is part of the encounter, moving us in redemptive ways from the world as it is to the world as it should be.

After learning more about the relational meeting, I would model such a meeting with one of the members of your group and then invite them to break up in pairs and engage a relational meeting themselves. In modeling this meeting, there are two things to remember: listening is as important as talking, and asking the right questions is critical. Here is a summary of what Ed Chambers says about questions:

In relational meetings, the "why" questions so often avoided by people have a space in which to surface: Why are things like they are; why am I doing what I do; why don't I spend more time on the things I say are most important to me? . . . Short succinct questions are the best: "Why do you say that;" "what does that mean to you;" "why do you care;" "have you ever tried to do anything about it?"[14] You must be prepared to interrupt with a brief, tight question like these, to then shut up and listen, and finally to share some things about yourself.[15]

Finally, see if your leadership group would be willing to commit to conducting a relational meeting campaign over a specific period of time (e.g., for six months), providing enough time for meetings to take place. Then invite ten or so of your leaders to conduct five to ten relational meetings each with congregants during this period. A concluding essential step is to ask each person conducting the meetings to write down a few notes on what they learned, recording such items as animating stories and passions, interests, leadership skills and qualities that emerge, and ways in which the person interviewed is acting (or willing to act) on their passions. At the end of the designated period, reconvene the group to share what they have learned and to reflect together on implications for the life and ministry of the whole congregation and the community around it. I think you will find that a relational meeting campaign will bear fruit for years to come!

Let me also offer a few thoughts on how to make relational meetings part of the day in, day out lifeblood of your church. As a part of my ministry, I try to do one or two relational meetings every week. It doesn't always happen (tasks get in the way!), but my intention is to make relational meetings part of the soul of my ministry. I do them with new members, older members, and all the people in between. I try to focus on leaders but intentionally engage others in the hope that leadership will emerge. It is also a good idea to have a cadre of folk (such as your governing board; cf. chapter 4) who have also committed to conducting such meetings on a regular basis. The group does not have to be large—remember Jesus had only twelve disciples! The importance of making relational meetings part of your life together is that they can transform a task-oriented church into a relational (or covenantal) community. The latter is much more powerful, for it can be the means for achieving many tasks. Blessings on your covenant journeys!

Postscript

In any community, there is a tension between a task-oriented culture and a relational (or covenantal) culture. Both are integral to a healthy community.

Tasks need the organizational structures of committees, agendas, and regulated, efficient actions. And actions, committees, and structures need to be grounded in, and responsive to, dynamic covenant relationships that are always in process. Most communities, however, have an overwhelming tendency to focus on tasks and structures, and the churches I have served are no exception to this rule. The New York Avenue Presbyterian Church, for example, is awash in tasks, such as serving the homeless and the mentally ill, tutoring inner-city teenagers, and tending to our members. We expend an enormous amount of energy engaging these tasks. In fact, tasks consume most of our time and energy. Thus, relationship building is not easy because it is most often done in and around our activities (our tasks). All of this is to say that relation building, if it is to be foundational to communal life, must be intentional and focused, for tasks can be all-consuming.

Thus, after our initial foray into relational building by means of the relational meeting campaign, we should not have been surprised to find how easy it was to lapse once again into a preoccupation with our many tasks and their structural supports. It happens! And yet something had changed, because a group of people had experienced the power of covenant making in the relational meeting. Thus, in 2013, our governing board (the session) initiated a process of covenanting together to do relational meetings with congregants each month (I will describe this process in chapter 4). During that time, we also had a fortuitous opportunity: a visiting community organizer, Stephan Baskerville, an organizer with West London Citizens in London, was assigned by the Washington Interfaith Network to work at New York Avenue for one month, during which he conducted thirty relational meetings with various leaders in the church. We then convened these thirty folk (most of them had not been involved in the original relational meeting campaign) for a night of training very similar to that described above in the practicum of this chapter. The energy in the room was so palpable that we each committed to doing three relational meetings with folk of our choosing over a six-week period. The goal, once again, was to forge vision, generate energy, discern gifts for ministry both within and outside the community, and to continue to build a relational culture within the church.

In my Reformed heritage, we affirm that the church is always reforming. Indeed, covenantal communities are dynamic and always in need of reform. So if we are truly to become a covenantal community, we need to be accountable to one another and to God for focused and intentional relationship building in order to counterbalance and fund the many tasks of the church and to inspire new ones. I guess you could say that one needs to institutionalize relation building but then let the relational culture reform the institution. The

Latin phrase for this is: *"Ecclesia reformata, semper reformanda,"* that is, "The church reformed, always reforming."

Finally, it is important to note that I continually encouraged folk to bring the relational meetings into a transformational conversation with their Christian faith. For example, I described the relational meeting as "an Easter pattern of dying and rising." In terms of the cruciform covenant that I described in the introduction, a relational meeting is covenanting with another at the intersection where God is bringing life out of broken places. But however it is described, for people of faith, it is a movement from insularity toward community and enables us to grow more deeply together into love of God, neighbor, and self.

Chapter 3

Engaging Covenant Community

The Great Commandment and the Listening Campaign

Every Sunday during worship, after leading the congregation in the Confession of Sin, I move to the baptismal font and remind them that their baptism is a sign and assurance of God's mercy and love. Then I invite those who are able to stand as a symbolic expression of restoration to right-standing with God and to hear the exhortation of the Great Commandment: "You shall love the Lord your God with all your heart, and with all your soul, and with all your mind, and with all your strength," and "You shall love your neighbor as yourself." I am always struck by the attentiveness of the congregation during these moments of confession, assurance of forgiveness, and exhortation and also by the varied circumstances of the people before me. On any given Sunday at The New York Avenue church, the worshiping congregation includes the homeless, visitors from across the country who have traveled to the nation's capital for conferences or tourism, and a diverse membership. Members themselves are at varied stages in their personal lives and in their journey with the church and have been drawn to the life of an urban congregation for any number of reasons. Thus it is a recurring moment in which I am keenly aware of two challenges before us—both of them challenges of "integration." The first is the challenge of living into the Great Commandment—a commandment that calls for the integration of heart, mind, and will as we embody love of God and neighbor and that thus has as its goal the wholeness or integrity of our lives of faith. Engaging the whole self in ministry is not easy, but it is not a solo venture. Indeed, it requires integration also into the life and ministry of a Christian community—the second challenge. How can we facilitate the genuine engagement and investment in shared ministry of such a diverse group of people, which includes relatively new members and longtime members, young and old, from varied quarters of a vast metropolitan region, with different needs, concerns, and gifts?

45

In this chapter, I want to reflect on daunting challenges of integration and introduce another organizing tool, "the listening campaign," which builds upon the one-on-one relational meetings of the previous chapter by broadening the conversation—engaging the whole community in collective discernment of the movement of God in its midst and directions in which it is being summoned as it seeks corporate embodiment of love of God and neighbor. Communal listening facilitates collective discernment and is a means by which we can integrate and engage our people in shared purpose and ministry.

The Commandment

There are a few places where I regularly see the glory of God's handiwork proclaimed. Following the Celts, I would call such locales "thin places," that is, places where the veil between this world and the other world (or what I would call time and eternity, the transcendent and immanent) are transparent. One of them for me is Colorado's Rocky Mountain National Park. I first encountered the magical world of the mountains when I was five, barely able to navigate a boulder let alone hike to the park's higher peaks. I find the mountains to be a place where I am especially drawn to contemplative prayer, as well as hiking. A few years ago, while browsing in my favorite hiking store in the nearby town of Estes Park, Colorado, I came across a hiking stool. It brought to mind all the descriptions in the Gospels of how often Jesus would retire to a quiet place, often a mountain, to sit and pray—and I thought, this is what I need for prayer—a stool to carry with me to a secluded mountain place. I purchased the stool and toted it to an amazing spot at the junction of two mountain streams, where, in blessed solitude, I pondered the glory of God in creation and what it might mean for me to glorify God in my life and ministry.

It was not lost on me that the stool upon which I was sitting at the confluence of those two mighty flowing streams was not only very lightweight and portable but also had three legs, all of which were connected by a single rubber ring. So as I was praying, Jesus' Great Commandment came to mind: "The first is, 'Hear, O Israel: the Lord our God, the Lord is one; you shall love the Lord your God with all your heart, and with all your soul, and with all your mind, and with all your strength.' The second is this, 'You shall love your neighbor as yourself.' There is no other commandment greater than these" (Mark 12:29–31). As I've noted previously, the three legs of the stool have become a model for me of the whole of the religious life conveyed by the Great Commandment: the life of the heart (or the contemplative life), the mind (or intellect) and the will (or one's activity). In corporate terms, those three legs also came to represent for me the church's worship or spiritual life (the life of the heart), its educational life (the life of the mind), and its socially-engaged and justice-seeking life (the life of the will). The three legs of my portable stool are connected by a rubber ring that stabilizes the whole, just as the integration of heart, mind, and will sustain the Christian life. Thus the stool in its entirety represents the whole integrated self and community as it lives in relation to God and neighbor.

The Great Commandment summarily combines two commandments that are to be observed simultaneously: love of God (Deut. 6:4–5) and love of neighbor (Lev. 19:18). This dual commandment is not unique to Jesus. As Amy-Jill Levine notes, the combination of love of God and love of neighbor appears in other early Jewish writings as a single commandment (e.g., "Love the Lord with all your life, and another with a sincere heart" in the *Testament of Dan* 5:3).[1] In the Gospel of Mark, the first of the twin commandments begins with the Shema, the Hebrew word for "hear" or "listen": "Hear O Israel, the Lord is One." To this day, Jews are to repeat the Shema twice daily, in the morning and in the evening. Many commentators note the connection in this commandment between monotheism ("the Lord is one") and our undivided love for God ("you shall love the Lord your God with all your heart, and with all your soul, and with all your mind, and with all your strength").[2] Integrity or wholeness, the engagement of heart, mind, and strength, activated by our love of both God and neighbor, is thus the goal of the commandment.

In the Sermon on the Mount in Matthew, Jesus makes a special appeal to wholeness when he calls for a "greater righteousness" and makes rather severe statements like "you must be perfect" (5:20). The Greek word translated "perfect" is *teleios*, which refers to completion or wholeness. Thus, when Jesus says, "you must be perfect," the point is *not* that disciples are to be sinless, but rather that they are to be single-hearted or undivided in their doing of the will of God. The opposite of this for Matthew's Jesus is hypocrisy, which means being divided in one's loyalty and devotion to doing the will of God. Jesus is interested in our basic attitudes and in the orientation of our whole selves—our actions, our feelings, our desires, the workings of our imaginations—toward love of God and love of neighbor. He is talking about the full investment of the total self, and that includes the subjective, affective side of who we are as well as our actions, our concrete behavior. It is a daunting challenge, but fortunately we do not do it alone. It is one we undertake in the company of a supportive community of faith that also seeks integration of heart, mind, and will in shared ministry. And careful listening is crucial on this front as well if we are to discern the movement of God among us. Careful listening helps us learn ways in which we might gather our energies for collective participation in God's work of mending the creation in the community around us. To that we now turn.

Listening

The integration of heart, mind, and will in our practice of love of God and neighbor is incumbent not only on the individual Christian but also on the community of faith. This, too, is a daunting challenge, for no church finds a perfect balance of the spiritual life (the life of the heart), the educational life (the life of the mind), and the socially-engaged and justice-seeking life (the life of the will). Moreover, a common assumption shared by many churches is that existing ministries have been established by divine decree (or by a church governing body) long ago and members (old and new) simply need to fit into existing patterns. It is remarkable how many of our ministries survive for years without anyone questioning whether or not they are still serving the purpose they once served or whether they continue to serve the goal of increasing love of God and neighbor. Yet any good community organizer will tell you that we should not make too many assumptions about such things. Before we act, it is crucial for members of a congregation to listen to one another and to the community around them in order to discern and engage appropriate communal practices. This has proved to be especially important in a transient and political urban setting like Washington, D.C., where new members—especially among the young adult population—arrive and others depart to pursue education, government service, or professional opportunities in different locations on a regular basis. Thus, as persons with different gifts, needs, and visions become part of the congregational journey, listening becomes all the more important. Moreover, taking the time to listen to what members think about the congregation's ministry is itself an embodiment of the Great Commandment in that when we listen to one another, we are respecting others as neighbors and thus loving them. Listening is also a means by which we discern how to balance our lives and ministry, for listening can help integrate the needs, gifts, and visions of the individual into the collective life and vision of a community of faith. In short, listening itself is a crucial practice.

In Matthew 18:20, Jesus promises, "For where two or three are gathered in my name, I am there among them." Thus God in Christ is most present to us in communal discernment. The Great Commandment, after all, mandates loving the "neighbor," and our most present neighbors are those in our community of faith as well as those in the community around us. It is important not to overlook the fact that the first word of the Great Commandment is *Shema*—"hear" or "listen." As we listen for God's word in Christ as it emerges within our community of faith, we are more able to discern what God has called us to be and do. Indeed, as we engage in the process of listening and discernment, the reality of God's grace precedes and empowers us, and what God is calling us together to be and do is discerned collectively in a Christ-formed community. This brings me to the importance of a "listening campaign" in a community of faith.

Listening is the heart and soul of communal life, but we do not do it often enough. Just as tasks often trump relational meetings, so too can the implementation of the many ministries of a church consume our time and attention, with the result that members engaged in those ministries are not consulted about them. How might we create space in our common life for listening? Community organizers use listening sessions to mobilize communities to address an injustice or a desperate need in a city or neighborhood. Listening sessions are often built on relational meetings and usually address the common concerns that emerged from the relational meetings. Moreover, just like the relational meeting entails telling stories, so also listening sessions invites storytelling wherein mutual recognition, trust, and action can emerge. For example, listening sessions were the key to the story of the grocery store in chapter 1. Listening sessions can also be a good way for a church to organize itself, claim its identity, discern direction, and energize people for shared ministry.

The Listening Campaign

Many people have written about the loss of relationships in modernity. Robert Bellah and Robert Putnam, to name just a couple, have thoroughly documented the individualism, self-absorption, and narcissism that pervade our culture. Real conversation of the sort entailed in the relational meeting is a lost art. As community organizer Ernesto Cortes puts it, "the real conversations of engagement—of listening, and particularly of listening to the other person as another, as someone who has a different perspective, a different point of view, a different story or history—do not exist anymore."[3] However, Cortes goes on to note that local associations (like the church) can play an instrumental role in facilitating genuine communal conversation and engagement. He harkens back to Alexis de Tocqueville, one of the more astute early observers of American politics, who was impressed with the fact that American citizens exhibited great interest in national politics but even more impressed with local community associations like the church. Local communal power, Tocqueville said, is the antidote to the greed and inequality inherent in larger cultural and political institutions. And local communities are key to the healthy functioning of the larger politics of the country. As Cortes notes,

> Tocqueville thought that America's intermediate institutions—congregations, family, networks of political associations and voluntary associations—were foundational to the creation of the kind of political community requisite for a democratic life and republican virtue. He believed they were the glue of a relational culture that enabled and sustained our capacity to practice democratic politics.[4]

If the church exists in, with, against, and for the world (as I have argued), then it cannot avoid politics; indeed, it has an instrumental role to play in facilitating the common good and our growth as responsible citizens and neighbors. In theological terms, responsible citizenship is among our covenant responsibilities, and it is one of the ways in which we are responsive to the sovereign God of all creation. We seek the common good as a means by which we give expression to love of God and neighbor. This is a countercultural activity because, as Cortes puts it, "This culture tells us that we are individual consumers, not citizens; that we are individual customers and clients rather than neighbors and members of associations."[5] So, if culture drains us of our God-given capacity to be responsible and responsive citizens and neighbors to one another, a primary work of the church is to teach what it means to be a neighbor.

And being a neighbor begins with the sacred art of listening. I often tell my congregation that Presbyterians take Matthew 18:20 quite literally, which is why we spend a great deal of time in committee meetings! We believe that God is present when we make decisions in committees and duly elected boards. Indeed, we are instinctively allergic to any one individual making decisions for us. To be sure, our communal decision-making can sometimes be clouded by pettiness, crude partisanship, and polarization, but more often than not we truly experience the presence of the risen Christ in our gatherings as we seek to make decisions about what we are called to be and do. In like manner, H. Richard Niebuhr taught that in every encounter with another person there is a moment of self-transcendence, as we move out of our insularity in encounter with another who can expand our horizon. He adds that in every encounter or dialogue, there is a "third" party (God) involved, making it a trialogue. And that third party "does not come to rest until the total community of being is involved."[6]

Listening sessions expand the conversations initiated in the individual relational meetings, drawing the whole community into collective discernment of the movement of God in its midst and the ministries to which it is being summoned—ministries that embody the love of God and neighbor and help us live out our covenant relationships. Thus, in the summer of 2011, The New York Avenue Presbyterian Church embarked on a series of "listening sessions." What follows is a short article I wrote for our church newsletter to describe what we were doing.

Summer Listening Campaign

The session of The New York Avenue Presbyterian Church believes it is an opportune moment to check the pulse of the congregation. To this end, a number of us have been engaged in "relational meetings" with congregants over the past year. We've learned a great deal from these conversations. Now we want to widen the scope of these meetings by engaging a "listening campaign" in the summer months. Beginning on June 19, and continuing on June 26, July 10, 17, and 24, we will hold small group sessions for 45 minutes each after the 10 a.m. worship service. During each successive session, we will seek answers to five key questions: What is church for you, and why? What is your deep desire for The New York Avenue Presbyterian Church? What are you concerned about in the life of The New York Avenue Presbyterian Church? What is your deep desire for the larger community around us? And what are your concerns for the larger community around us? We will engage these questions in small groups. There will be a facilitator and note-taker for each group so that responses can be gathered for further reflection, and we hope and trust that the ideas, concerns, and desires that are expressed in these discussions will inform the future ministries of the church. I also plan to preach on these questions and will share some of what we learn in the group meetings in those sermons. We promise to conclude each of these five sessions promptly at 12 noon, so you will be free to depart for lunch with family or friends. Please plan to come and participate in what the session views an important series of conversations about our beloved community.

June 19: What is church for you, and why?

June 26: What is your deep desire for The New York Avenue Presbyterian Church? And what are you willing to do about it?

July 10: What are you concerned about in the life of The New York Avenue Presbyterian Church? And what are you willing to do about it?

July 17: What is your deep desire of the larger community around us? And what are you willing to do about it?

July 24: What are your concerns for the larger community around us? And what are you willing to do about it?[7]

The Book of Revelation and Holy Listening

It may strike some as odd that I chose to ground my preaching on these questions in the book of Revelation, so let me explain. I have become convinced that Revelation is a rich resource for reflection as we ponder the calling of the contemporary church in our world. In recent years, there has been a renaissance of scholarship on Revelation, and to some degree this resurgence of interest has been evoked by the striking similarities between the imperial backdrop of Revelation and our own present-day imperial reality.

The Roman Empire was the dominant political and military force of the world of the New Testament and a reality that changed everything for people who lived within its boundaries. As Richard Horsley notes,

> In extending its imperial rule over the whole Mediterranean world and its systematic exploitation of subject peoples and in Augustus's final 'pacification' of the whole world, Rome . . . thus established "a new world order," with itself as the only remaining superpower. . . . The more critical recent investigations of the principal politics and practices of Roman imperialism suggest that what was a "new world order" for those of power and privilege was experienced as a disruptive, disorienting, or even devastating new world *disorder* for many of the subject peoples.[8]

In short, the Romans may have brought peace to the empire but not peace of mind to its people, for it established a world in which the individual person had little direct control over his or her life. Moreover, the empire brooked no opposition. If you bucked the system you could be crucified, and thus most people felt powerless and obligated to accommodate themselves to the political, religious, and economic system, or else! And Christians living in the empire knew all too well what that "or else" entailed. The cross upon which their savior died was a constant reminder of Roman imperial power.

In like manner, many twenty-first-century Americans feel powerless and at the mercy of forces beyond their control. In the wake of the economic meltdown of 2008, people are still looking for someone to blame: greedy traders, misguided regulators, sleazy subprime lenders, kowtowing legislators, or clueless home buyers; thus begins the book *All the Devils Are Here*, the title of which comes from Shakespeare's *The Tempest*, which declares, "Hell is empty, and all the devils are here." The authors of the book conclude that the real culprits in the economic meltdown include all the above.[9] Whoever the devils and whatever their number, the net effect is joblessness that won't go away and cut, cuts, and more cuts in government programs for the poor simply because these cuts meet the least resistance. During recent budget negotiations by the D.C. City Council, one council member told the Washington Interfaith Network (the local IAF organization of which my church is a member) that the choice as he saw it was between cutting money for programs for the poor *or* cutting money for the homeless, because tax increases were out of the question. It's true: all the devils are here!

According to Revelation, we are among those devils unless we resist and agitate. In his commentary on Revelation, Brian Blount says that the gist of the message of this book is this: Christ is telling the seven churches to which Revelation is addressed to "pick a fight!"[10] To this end, Blount points out that the Greek word *hypomonē* that Revelation uses to describe this posture, often translated as "endurance," can and should be translated as "nonviolent resistance" and entails imitating Christ. Here is Blount's translation of Revelation 2:2, Christ's words to the Ephesian church: "I know your works, which are your struggle and your nonviolent resistance. Because you cannot bear evil people, you tested the ones who called themselves apostles but are not and you found them to be liars."[11] In Revelation, the test for truthfulness is the crucified Christ, or what I have previously called cruciformity. The cross of Christ is the interpretive lens through which they (and we) are called to view the world in order to unmask its deformities, defacements, and oppression. The cross is the lens by which we can discern what we are called to be and do in order to expand our personal and collective hearts so that we might truly live into the covenantal loves of the Great Commandment.

One comment that emerged in our first listening lesson, offered by a long-time member, really struck me. "I come here to get a shot in the arm to reorient myself in order to counter the world's values the rest of the week." This is exactly what Revelation prescribes as the work of the church—the work of inoculation for active, nonviolent resistance to the deformities of our world and the powers that produce them. Another way of saying this could employ Martin Luther King Jr.'s image of the Beloved Community: the work of the church is the work of loving the world into reconciliation with others and God so that the whole world can become the community of the reconciled and redeemed. Rowan Williams gives expression to the same end when he says this: "Jesus did not come to be "a competitor for space in the world." Rather, in his life, death, and resurrection "the human map is being redrawn, the world turned upside down," and as such, "the whole world of rivalry and defense" is put into question.[12]

Practically speaking, what does this mean? It means acting on our faith as people who are baptized in the crucified and risen Christ. This may mean, on the one hand, openly challenging hate language and ideologies, and, on the other hand, organizing people for change. Philosopher Jeffrey Stout borrows two metaphors from Henry David Thoreau to describe what is wrong and what needs to change in America: that of the "sleeper" and "uprising." The "sleeper," the metaphor for what is wrong, is a railroad term referring to the cross-ties upon which the rails are laid. Thoreau uses the term to refer to those upon whose backs political, economic, and social oppression runs. If they remain in a prone position, everything will run smoothly. And if the sleepers rise up one by one, they will be run over. If the system is to change, an "uprising" of sleepers is needed—sleepers who are "organized, coordinated, and self-aware."[13] This is precisely what Revelation envisions as the work of the church: it is to be a community of organized, active, nonviolent resistance. It follows the example of Jesus, who overturned the tables of money lenders in the temple and who calls his disciples to pick up their crosses and follow. Thus, in one of our listening lessons, when I was asked the question, "What do I desire most for The New York Avenue Church?", I responded, "I want us to pick a fight!"

Here is the sermon I preached, based on the book of Revelation, on the last Sunday of our listening campaign.

AN INDEPENDENT INITIATIVE

Revelation 7 and 21

In this final sermon on Revelation, I want to try to pull together the varied strands of this most enigmatic book of the Bible that we have been exploring these last weeks. As I've noted in the past weeks, recent scholarship on this book suggests that its purpose was to issue a wake-up call to churches of Asia Minor who had become way too cozy with the Roman Empire—way too accommodating and tolerant of its abusive practices, which included the exploitation of people and nature. Barbara Rossing, for example, points to Revelation 18 for a detailed listings of the natural and human resources that Rome was extracting from its colonies. The reality of empire proved to be an ecological and human nightmare and, accordingly, Revelation depicts Rome as a seven-headed beast—each head representing one of the Caesars. This image functioned in many respects as a political cartoon aimed to startle the churches into recognition of the fearsome political beast to which they were accommodating—to startle them out of their complacency. Indeed, Brian Blount contends that Revelation is imploring the churches in these colonies to "pick a fight" with the empire. This fight to which Christians were called, according to Blount, was not one of violence but of nonviolent resistance, along the lines embodied in the civil rights movement and the teaching of Martin Luther King Jr. Revelation speaks of the power of such nonviolent resistance as "lamb power," which gives expression to the theology of the cross—a nonviolent resistance and witness that unmasks and exposes oppression and exploitation for what it is: an abusive defacement and betrayal of God's intent for the creation. Lamb power conquers by loving what God loves and thereby unmasking the idolatries of the world. Lamb power also holds together God's judgment and mercy, love and justice. The ultimate vision of Revelation 21—the new Jerusalem coming down from heaven—is that of justice for victims; yet implicit in this vision is the hope that the enemy, the oppressor, will overhear the words of judgment and repent. The final vision of Revelation is, thus, transformative of all creation.

This final vision of the new Jerusalem is very much akin to Martin Luther King Jr.'s vision of the Beloved Community. King's core theological vision was profoundly one of reconciliation in which both love and justice were held together. He perceived how hate cripples and destroys the oppressor as well as the victim. King believed that the sovereign love of God was the ruling power of the universe. Thus our love for others is not simply a warm feeling but rather love extended for the purpose of reconciling that which is estranged from God. King repeatedly contended that the civil rights movement was the struggle for liberation of black America and the redemption of the soul of all Americans. The goal was the creation of the Beloved Community.[14] And if this is the goal, nonviolent resistance is the only moral and practical means to this end. But this leaves us with the question: What can we do to further this goal in our own time and place? What might nonviolent resistance based in lamb power look like on our corner of Washington, D.C.? It is the practical question that hangs over the book of Revelation.

Theologian Susan Thistlethwaite stimulates our imaginations, inviting us to consider possibilities, I think, in her book on interfaith peacemaking when she identifies one of the principles of just peacemaking as this: "taking independent initiative" to deescalate violence and create a climate that can be transformative. For example, during the war in Bosnia in the early 1990s, Muslim students were expelled from their homes and colleges by Serbian fighters and by Catholic Christians. So not only were they targets of racial and ethnic hostility; they also could not continue their education. When the U. S. Fellowship of Reconciliation (FOR), a nonprofit organization, found out about the students and their circumstance, they decided to take the initiative. First, they had to get the students safely out of harm's way, and then they had to convince Christian colleges in the United States to educate students without documentation and without charging them tuition. Finally, they had to find families who would provide lodging and support for these students. They were able to secure the safety of 150 Bosnian students, to transport them to the U.S., and to house them with families so that they could continue their education. Thus these Muslim students, who had been victimized by "Christians" in their homeland, now found themselves in reconciling relationships with Christians, as well as Jews and Muslims, across the United States. The impact of this project was immense. Doug Hostetter of FOR describes it this way:

> The project not only saved the lives of scores of excellent students, it also gave Americans something positive to do in the face of an overwhelming tragedy. . . . [It] offered American Christians an opportunity to distance themselves from the triumphalist tradition of the "Christian" armies of the [Crusades in the] Middle Ages and enabled them to identify with a much older Judea-Christian tradition of hospitality, compassion, and love as practiced by the Patriarchs, Christ, and the apostolic church. It was a great shock to many students who had been driven from their homes by "Christian" armies in Bosnia to see that the families and schools that gave them love, shelter, and education in the U.S were also Christian.[15]

After the project began, Doug Hostetter went to Bosnia to visit the families of the students now studying in the U.S. He took along photos of them for their families, who had not seen them for years. He also photographed the families for their homesick children in the U.S. Hostetter says this about the experience: "The tears of joy and pain on both sides of the Atlantic were almost too much to absorb. One mother explained, 'You have been the face of God to us at a time when the whole world seems to have turned its back on the Bosnian people.'"[16]

Hostetter and the FOR did more than oppose violence. They took an initiative that would promote just peacemaking. And what a huge difference it made for 150 Bosnian students and their families, and for thousands of Americans who got to know these students and their personal stories. The seeds of peace and reconciliation were sown in all these people in a way that would have lasting impact. And time will tell how those students, upon returning to their country, might impact the future direction of their postwar nation.

Few of us have been subject to the kind of violence suffered by the people of Bosnia. But all of us, in one way, shape, or form, can find ourselves in polarized circumstances—with respect to race, gender, class, religion, ethnicity, or politics. How could we not, for we live in a polarized nation and world. What, then, should we do? The biblical counsel is this: use your imagination and take the initiative!

The listening session that will take place immediately after today's service will provide an opportunity for us to exercise our imaginations and think together about initiatives we might want to engage on the near horizon, for the question before us will be this: *What are your concerns for the larger community around us? And what are you willing to do about it?* Here are some things, for example, that I find myself pondering. One thing I'm concerned about is jobs; and so I've been wondering, What could we do about it? Our federal government appears deadlocked, as our political parties remain polarized over federal spending when they ought to be attending to what America needs most—jobs, and good jobs in particular. So how might we hold our public officials accountable? Clearly, the infrastructure is falling apart—roads and bridges, for example, and a public works jobs program would put people back to work, put money back into the economy, increase revenue, and reduce the deficit. Could we, perhaps, in partnership with others, find a way to promote job programs in connection with public works desperately needed in the District of Columbia?

There are plenty of other matters that might deeply concern us. Washington, D.C., to mention but one more obvious example, is arguably the most economically and racially polarized city in the nation—with a growing white, black, and Asian-American middle and upper-middle class population and a largely black working class population in Wards 7 and 8, where there is 20-percent unemployment. What could we do? On this front we are actually embarking on a new initiative in the months ahead. New York Avenue is partnering with two neighboring black churches to engage together in study and extended conversation about race and poverty, which is tearing this city apart. Will this partnership, this face-to-face conversation over the course of months or years, be awkward? Yes. But it is worth it if it can make a constructive contribution, in this city at least, to depolarization on the one hand and transformation on the other.

Every one of us faces polarized circumstances of some sort or another everywhere we turn, and if I am understanding Revelation correctly, it is imploring us to use our imaginations and take some initiative, empowered by the One who first took the initiative for us, revealing the God whose way in the world is cruciform, who is always about transformation, about reconciling the estranged, about creating the Beloved Community of the Lamb.

The vision of the new Jerusalem with which Revelation concludes is a vision of the future God intends for us all. It is an urban vision of a city filled with the glory of God in which all have access to the good gifts of creation—the river of the water of life, and the tree of life, with twelve fruits and leaves for the healing of the nations. It is the direction in which we are moving, and the basis for any and all initiatives we may claim as our calling in this time and place—initiatives based on a hopeful vision of the day when there will be no more tears, no more death, and no more pain. And this final vision of Revelation and the Bible is no pie in the sky optimism, because it is grounded in the very earthiness of one who was crucified and was raised by God from the dead—the lamb who now sits upon the throne and who summons us to follow his same earthy and cruciform path—and *to take the initiative*!

Amen.

Listening and Practice

What emerged from the listening sessions in which the congregation engaged over the course of two months? Insights that emerged from the sessions can be grouped in three basic areas. First, we learned a great deal about the impact of NYAPC on members' lives. Here are some of the statements members made about that: I am "able to take Scripture from worship and apply it in my daily life"; I "like the Radcliffe Room ministry [NYAPC's homeless ministry]—it says a lot about the church's values, and I want to raise my daughter here so that she will experience these values"; "I didn't grow up in the church so I'm behind the eight-ball in spiritual formation, but I hope to catch up on that in the next few years"; "people know you warts and all and love you warts and all and challenge you"; NYAPC is a "place to be challenged to grow and a place to search and serve"; it is a "place to learn from the homeless people who are nearby."

Second, we learned a great deal about relationships within the church from comments about them. For example, many found the relational meetings to be a significant experience—one that was playing an important role in changing the culture of the church from an agenda and task orientation to a relational one. Others articulated a desire for more small groups, for revitalization of the young adults' group, and for more intergenerational activities.

Third, there was a good bit of discussion of our ministries and of the limits of our financial resources to address them. For instance, one person observed that "we can't respond to opportunities because we lack resources to pay for current needs." Others strongly urged the leadership of the church to do a more creative job balancing finances, resources, and ministry.

Moreover, there were a variety of outcomes from this campaign. Let me mention three of them. The first was its impact on our young adult ministry. The New York Avenue Church has been blessed over the years with a large and growing contingent of young adults who actively participate in the life of the church. This is due, in part, to the demographics of Washington, D.C., and the real need young adults have to connect to one another and to a larger intergenerational community. However, Washington is in many respects a transient city, particularly for this age group, and thus the group is always in flux as some leave town because of professional opportunities or far-flung government service, others go back to school, and still others become disillusioned with the politics of the city and leave. The listening campaign gave our young adults an opportunity to speak about the larger life of the church and to contribute their input to collective reflection about the church's direction. Moreover, they engaged in their own listening sessions to discern their role within the church. The result was an organized effort for expanded fellowship opportunities within the group (e.g., happy hours for theological conversations) and even greater participation within the boards and ministries of the church.

A second outcome of the listening campaign pertains to the financial condition of the church. Feedback during the sessions expressed a clear concern for addressing the church's pressing financial needs. Subsequent to the campaign, the Finance Committee organized an initiative to discern creative ways in which the church can move towards greater fiscal responsibility. Heretofore, we had been drawing on our endowments in order to cover shortfall. The long and short of it is that the church's heart is bigger than its wallet, so something had to be done. A questionnaire went out to each board and the answers to the questions became part of a working document that the session (the governing board) of the church adopted as a working plan to resolve our financial issues. Then, in the summer of 2012, we conducted three more listening sessions around these questions to follow up on financial concerns: When have you experienced abundance in the midst of scarcity? How have church, family and culture influenced how you think about money? What moves you to give of yourself, your time, your resources? How are church and charity different? As a result of these initiatives, we have begun to cut our deficits and are now on our way toward a sustainable budget.

Finally, a renewed focus on spiritual growth within the congregation emerged from the listening campaign, about which I will say more in the next chapter. Suffice it to say here that we discerned that we needed to act on the spiritual yearnings that were being expressed amid our many activities—that this was an aspect of our life that was "out of balance," in need of focused attention.

In sum, it has seemed to me that there has been a renewal of energy in all of our ministries since we began the relational meetings and the listening sessions. In fact, someone recently said to me that, in all the time she had been a member here, she had never seen such vitality in the life of the church! If so, then we are moving ever closer to fulfilling the very purpose of the church: increasing love of God and neighbor: in other words, living the Great Commandment.

Practicum

In this chapter, we explored the countercultural activity of embracing our calling as a covenant community by engaging in the sacred art of listening. In this practicum, let me offer suggestions about how you might organize such a campaign. Below is a model that was engaged by the Takoma Park Presbyterian Church in Takoma Park, Maryland:

Finding our Voice:
Listening, Forming Friendships, Acting on our Common Faith

TPPC 2011 Listening Campaign, February to May 2011

Why have a "listening campaign" in Takoma Park Presbyterian Church?
To deepen the "relational culture" of the congregation so that we can act powerfully together on our common faith.

What concrete result will come of our discussion?
We will create a new list of mission priorities reflecting our common calling. This will help us set goals and create a budget for 2012.

How will we listen to one another?
One Sunday a month, February to May, we will have "small group conversations" in worship. Each Sunday will focus on one question. We will open with 30 minutes of worship and then 45 minutes of discussion in small groups or come during the week to share and listen.

Worship Format for the Sunday Mornings
   Keep worship to 30 minutes
     No Announcements
     Welcome and Call to Worship
     1 Hymn
     Time with Children
     Scripture Reading and Explaining the Day's Question
     Prayers
     Offertory
   Brief Prayer and Benediction

Calendar and Discussion Question

February 13   *"What is church for you? Why?"*
or come on Feb. 15 from 7:30 to 8:30 for a small group discussion (parlor)

February 20   *Sermon reflects on what we shared*

March 13   *"What is your deep desire for the life of TPPC?"*
or come March 14 from 7:30 to 8:30 for a small group discussion (parlor)

March 27   *Sermon reflects on what we shared*

April 10   *"What are you so concerned about in our larger community that you personally are willing to act on it? Why?"*
or come April 11 from 7:30 to 8:30 for a small group discussion (parlor)

April 17   *Sermon reflects on what we shared*

May 8   *Summary review of what we heard for feedback and revision*
or come May 9 from 7:30 to 8:30 for a small group discussion (parlor)

May 15   *Sermon reflects on what we've learned.*

June 14	*Session meets to creates a new list of mission priorities for our church*
Autumn	*Session present goal budget for 2012, based on what we've learned.*

The nuts and bolts of a listening campaign can vary. Takoma Park's model is self-contained within the worship experience. The listening sessions we have conducted at New York Avenue were held immediately after worship on a succession of Sundays. Our format was as follows: We gathered our members into groups of no more than eight or nine, each with a convener and note taker. Each session was devoted to one question, moderated by the convener. The sessions lasted forty-five minutes and were promptly concluded at noon. We then compiled the notes of each meeting, which were then summarized and reported back to the congregation. I reflected on the notes each week and factored them into my preaching preparation.

Whatever model you choose to follow, I heartily commend the practice of listening sessions as a means by which to deepen relationships within your community and to discern new directions for ministry. There are many different kinds of listening sessions that a congregation could engage with the community around it. They might come out of relational meetings that your church has conducted in the community around a common issue of concern. The grocery store story that began this book is one such example. The jobs initiative that I will address in chapter 7 is another.

Listening is a holy activity wherein we respect others as images of the glory of the living God. James 1:19 advises that we "be quick to listen, slow to speak, slow to anger." This is good and holy advice for people who seek to live in covenant relationships with others and with God.

Chapter 4

Deepening Covenant Community

The Contemplative

In the preceding chapter, I mentioned that one of the places where I regularly see the glory of God's handiwork is in Colorado's Rocky Mountain National Park. I mentioned the hiking stool upon which I love to sit at an amazing spot at the junction of two mountain streams that merge to become the Big Thompson Canyon River. I want to share a good bit more about what happened to me at the juncture between those two mountain streams—an epiphany of sorts—as a means of getting at a vitally important resource for the personal and corporate religious life: the contemplative. I will explain what "the contemplative" means and share my understanding of it as a critical tool for urban life and ministry.

There is something uniquely symbolic about streams that merge into one that speak to me about God's intentions and purposes for us and for all of history. Indeed, one of the most striking features of the Bible is that a river runs through it. In the creation story with which the Bible begins we learn that "a river flows out of Eden to water the garden" (Gen. 2:10). That river eventually separates into the Tigris and Euphrates rivers that flowed through ancient Babylon (modern day Iraq), extending the hope of the blessing of the original creation to the whole world. Then, at the end of the Bible, in the final chapter of the book of Revelation, the vision of the new Jerusalem coming down from heaven also features a river: "The angel showed me the river of the water of life, bright as crystal, flowing from the throne of God and the Lamb through the middle of the street of the city (Rev. 22:1–2)." This vision symbolizes the restoration of the original blessing for the whole creation. And it is not insignificant that this restored blessing takes place in an urban setting.

Yet the rivers and waters of the biblical story symbolize more than blessing; they also symbolize chaos, retribution, and exploitation. For instance, the "sea" in the book of Revelation represents the means by which Rome colonizes its empire. Thus water can symbolize both blessing and curse. The same is true of American history. The sea that transported people to the New World and to freedom there in the hoped-for new Jerusalem also conveyed slaves from the African continent to the New World to till the fields. The rivers of the New World nourished the land but were eventually poisoned with chemicals from plants intentionally built near water to facilitate cheap waste disposal. Rivers and waters convey the Bible's story and that of all human history—a story of both blessing and conquest, an ambiguous story at best. But the fact that water continues to symbolize life, nourishment, and abundance amid brokenness and exploitation says a great deal about a God who refuses to give up on God's good creation. In other words, rivers and waters convey the cruciform story of Christian faith.

Nibbling and Crucifixion

What was the nature of the epiphany of sorts that I experienced at the juncture of those two mountain streams? To get at that, I need to draw on a baseball image that will be forever seared into my memory. My wife contends that I still haven't gotten over the last game of the 2012 baseball season for the Washington Nationals, and she's right—I haven't! You won't find a devoted Nats fan—even a casual Nats fan—who doesn't remember that game. It was the deciding game of the Divisional Series between the Nats and the St. Louis Cardinals; the winner would play in the National League Championship Series. The Nats got off to an amazing start, building a 6 to 0 lead in just the first few innings. But then the Cardinals slowly chipped away at that lead. Even so, the Nats could have won the game with just one more out in the ninth inning. In fact, all that they needed was one pitch, the right pitch, to get a final out. But they couldn't get it. The Cardinals got strategic hits to get on base, the Nats walked too many batters and couldn't get that last strike, that last out; and thus they lost the game. It was painful—so painful that I couldn't watch sports for a long time. Someone had to tell me who won the World Series in 2012 because I couldn't watch any of it! I'll never forget what the Nats manager, Davey Johnson, said after that painful loss that ended the season. He said this of the Nats pitchers: "They were nibbling, and it was painful to watch." By nibbling he meant that the Nats pitchers weren't challenging the batters with their best stuff: they were nibbling around the edge of the strike zone and throwing too many balls. So now we know what the pitching coach was saying to those pitchers when he went to the mound time and again toward the end of the game: "Stop nibbling!"

I suspect we all know what "nibbling" is. Nibbling is when our efforts are half-baked, lackluster, ill-conceived, and insufficient—when we are not putting forth our best stuff. Theologically, nibbling reflects halfhearted devotion to God and others. More ominously, it is the "lukewarm" state of the Laodicean congregation that Christ speaks of spitting out of his mouth in Revelation 3. Nibbling, in other words, is a halfhearted Christian faith that settles for less—for Band-Aids or charity—and equivocates in its witness to the cruciform God who resurrects life out of broken places. Nibbling is itself a symptom of our own brokenness, and there are signs of it all around us. Just two examples will suffice.

Consider, for example, the minimum wage and common assumptions about it. Much of the public and political discourse about it seems to assume that any job is better than no job even if the wages it provides cannot lift a person out of poverty. Yet a faith-informed understanding of work holds that every job should be a vocation, whether it entails trash collection or presiding as the CEO of a major company. God calls each of us to good work that contributes to the common good, which means work that builds community, that provides a living wage with benefits, and that promotes human dignity. And when such work is not available to all and we are not working for the day when it is then we're just nibbling, oblivious to crucifixions in our landscape.

Take another example: politics. Many people are disheartened by utter lack of civility in political discourse—by polarized, partisan, and disgustingly dirty politics, yet they doubt there is anything they can do to change it. A faith-informed understanding of citizenship would surely suggest that we have a birthright to reclaim as political people. By God's grace, we live in a free, democratic society and have the power to participate in the political process. We can hold our elected officials accountable, compelling them to put an end to partisanship and pursue the common good with legislation that provides good jobs, housing, health care for all, and protection for the consumer. We can promote the rebuilding of the infrastructure of our country, and maybe even the raising of taxes to support it, because politics should not have winning and losing as its goal but rather dedication to the common good at home and support for peacemaking efforts and economic opportunities abroad. Anything less is nibbling—and complicity with crucifixion.

There are, of course, many reasons why we might nibble. Perhaps we nibble because we are fearful, angry, or lost and can't find the way. We try this and that but never seem to stumble upon the right path. We are in need of direction. So bear with me while I wander just a bit into the Judean wilderness to consider John the Baptist's testimony to that fact, for he spoke words that I think we need to hear—words that evoke reflection on why and how we nibble:

> In the fifteenth year of the reign of Emperor Tiberius, when Pontius Pilate was governor of Judea, and Herod was ruler of Galilee, and his brother Philip ruler of the region of Ituraea and Trachonitis, and Lysanias ruler of Abilene, during the high priesthood of Annas and Caiaphas, the word of God came to John son of Zechariah in the wilderness. He went into all the region around the Jordan, proclaiming a baptism of repentance for the forgiveness of sins, as it is written in the book of the words of the prophet Isaiah,
>
>> "The voice of one crying out in the wilderness:
>> 'Prepare the way of the Lord,
>>   make his paths straight
>> Every valley shall be filled,
>>   and every mountain and hill shall be made low,
>> and the crooked shall be made straight,
>>   and the rough ways made smooth;
>> and all flesh shall see the salvation of God.'"
>>
>> (Luke 3:1–6)

Luke's vision in this scene is staggering in its breadth, for it begins with the Roman Emperor in its purview. It then cycles downward from the wealth and political might of Rome, sketching increasingly narrower circles around local political functionaries in Judea and Galilee until it draws a bead on the scruffy figure of John the Baptist in the desolate wilderness. This suggests, I think, that our own vision of the world should include the highest places and the lowest places—the skyscrapers and penthouses of big business and finance as well as the desolate ghettoes in most of our inner cities. My own ministry context requires such a breadth of vision, for it comprises two different cities, both named Washington, D.C.: there is the Washington of the highly professional elite who flock here from varied parts of the country and there is the Washington of its native citizens, those born and bred in a city that many feel has given up on them. Indeed, Luke's vision is poignantly relevant to urban churches because 79 percent of the U.S. population, with all its diversity, resides in metropolitan areas (similar percentages apply to urban centers worldwide). And because Luke's Gospel (among all the Gospels) is particularly attentive to realities of economic and social disparity, it is especially sensitive to injustices suffered by those on the margins of society. The problem is not only economic and painfully material but also spiritual, which is to say that it is a problem that bears on the condition of our hearts—hearts that reflect the deformations of the world. Luke's Mary speaks of this condition when she predicts that the coming savior will "scatter the proud in the imagination of their hearts" (Luke 1:51).

Augustine, too, spoke of this condition, defining the spiritual poison that infuses our hearts as pride. Theologian Wendy Farley, while not denying Augustine's diagnosis of our condition, goes further when she says:

> I suspect that deeper than any pride we suffer is the anguished uncertainty that we deserve happiness. History tells those on its "underside" how worthless and impotent they are. But those who dwell in history's penthouse apartments carry the worm of self-doubt within them as well. We require the trappings of wealth and power because it is too hard to believe that permanent, stable, inexhaustible happiness belongs to us.[1]

What Farley is describing is a spiritual problem—a problem of the heart. We are all beloved of God, created to be vessels of God's own image and thereby to glorify God in all that we are and do. But in our spiritual core, we don't believe it. Reinhold Niebuhr said it differently but pointed to the same root problem when he wrote, "the ideal possibility is that faith in the ultimate security of God's love would overcome the immediate insecurities of nature and history." Yet insecurity reigns. And so he describes our fundamental sin as "unbelief."[2] A good baseball coach will tell you that a pitcher "nibbles" because he doesn't "trust his stuff"—he is insecure, for instance, about his change-up or his curveball. So, too, we nibble because we don't trust the stuff that holds us in life; in short, we don't trust God's love. At its core, nibbling is insecurity that can manifest itself in fear, anxiety, anger, or an incessant meandering because we've lost our way. Luke uses various metaphors to describe this plight. Drawing from Isaiah's message to the exiles in ancient Babylon, he speaks of valleys that need lifting, mountains that need leveling, and meandering paths that need to be made straight.

Flannery O'Connor was an astute observer of the human condition and the spiritual problem at the heart of it. If you've ever read her classic short story "A Good Man is Hard to Find," then you will no doubt remember the overbearing grandmother who is its central character—who, on a family road trip, takes her family in meandering directions. At her insistence, after considerable nagging, they end up taking a detour down an unfortunate dirt road to see a place she recalls from her childhood. But along the way, the car swerves off the road and lands them in a ditch. When a man stops, presumably to help, she delivers one of her classic lines: she says to the man, "We're in a real predicament here, a real predicament." She has no idea how much of a predicament, for it turns out that the man she is talking to is an escaped convict, and the story does not have a happy ending. It's an apt description for the human condition, for we are all, in one way, shape, or form, in a real predicament, stuck in a ditch, seeking help from people who are themselves prisoners on the run. We're in a real predicament, at the mercy of various culprits—fear, anger, and existential angst among them.

All of us have found ourselves at one time or another stuck in ditches of fear or chronic anxiety that paralyze us, deflate our sense of worth, and inhibit our actions.[3] They can shut us down, making even simple acts of compassion—of connection with others—enormously difficult. Indeed, we can be so imprisoned by fear and anxiety that we struggle with basic human ethical inclinations such as the one Paul Ricoeur identifies with the words "you too, like me."[4] Or sometimes anger, even rage, takes us hostage. We can find ourselves buried under mountains of anger—evoked by the conflicts that mar our family life and work environments as well as interminable wars that mark out time.

For many of us, though, the predicament is not simply a ditch of fear or mountain of rage but rather an incessant meandering. As a wise cultural critic once observed, "In the kindergarten of contemporary culture, the big gold stars are given out for being open, tentative and provisional. We are into that and into this but the ease of our entrances and exits betrays the fact that in the end we're not much into anything at all. We are akin to what we say to the salesperson in the department store 'Just looking.'"[5] There is a yearning deep inside of us: it is a yearning to love God, others, and ourselves, a yearning that reflects the image of God in us—yet we continue to meander, in exile from the love that God intends for us.

In short, we're in a real predicament here—for a number of reasons! But the good news of the gospel, of course, is that we are not left to our own devices. God has not left us in the ditch or buried under mountains or meandering in exile. Incarnation is God's response to our predicament. Incarnation is about God coming close, becoming flesh, fully experiencing our utter fear, rage, and meandering. Indeed, the cruciform wounds of Christ show us where the divine love is present: it is present in our wounds, our terror, our rage, and our existential angst, seeking to set us free from them and empowering us to love.

The importance of incarnation—God's coming close—was impressed upon me on one of my hiking vacations. My wife and I took an out-of-the-way hike in the backwoods of British Columbia in the Mount Robson Provincial Park. We had trouble even finding the trailhead. But we found something resembling a trail of sorts and hiked some four hours through dense woods and up a fairly sizable mountain. However, on our way back down the mountain, we came to a spot where the trail just ended. We backtracked a bit and found another trail that seemed to be heading down and followed it for a while, but it also dead-ended. For almost an hour we looked and looked for the trail, but we couldn't find it. Ominously, the thickets all around us were teeming with wild berries, and bears just love wild berries! We were lost and alone and feeling very vulnerable, even a little bit frantic. But then something caught our attention: the footprint of a hiking boot, deeply imprinted in a marsh that was about twenty yards long. When my wife saw the imprint, she climbed to the top of a rocky area to see what was on the other side of the marsh, and spotted the trail that would lead us home. And the interesting thing about that footprint in the mud is that it was pointing in our direction—it was headed toward us! Here is what may sound like a crazy idea, but it is the gospel truth: that the God of the universe cares enough about a wayward people to search the breadth and depth of creation to uncover every stone until each and every one of us is found.

Admittedly I have been meandering a bit in my thoughts to this point, into ditches, up mountains, and along crooked paths that reflect something of our human spiritual predicament! However, I believe it is crucial to traverse this terrain if we are to grasp the fundamental importance of "the contemplative." Wendy Farley defines the contemplative as the "conscious desire to enter more deeply into the divine Eros that flows through all things. . . . Through contemplation, shifts can gradually occur in the body, in the emotions and in understandings, beliefs, vocations, and relationships. Transformation of desire slowly manifests in every aspect of our being." Moreover, Farley contends that "attention to our interiority deepens our capacity for justice. Or rather, it roots justice in the well-spring of compassion."[6] In short, the contemplative entails both personal and corporate prayer and worship, and it creates the space in which we find release from fear, rage, and incessant meandering and discover our yearning for God and God's yearning for us. Moreover, the contemplative is a space in which we discover passion for justice and love of neighbor as self, for it facilitates our discernment of God's will. The contemplative creates the space in which we begin to discern the cross-shaped realities in the landscape around us, where God may be at work bringing life out of brokenness and summoning our participation in the divine work of mending the creation. Such discernment is essential—foundational—to the Christian life.

The contemplative is mightily important to the life of faith, but it is shocking how little time many Christians devote to it. Most of us wouldn't dream of missing three meals a day, but attending to contemplative practice is sometimes an afterthought at best. In other words, when it comes to the contemplative life itself, we nibble!

If you have managed to hang in there with me while I've roamed the topography of the human predicament, now I can finally tell you what happened at the juncture of those two mountain streams in the Rocky Mountain National Park. It didn't happen in a single moment, but over a period of two weeks of prayer, during which I became ever more aware that something was restlessly stirring in my life. It is hard to express in words, but here is my best attempt: What rose to the surface was awareness of the fearful, angry, and meandering streams of my life and of those within my community of faith. An awareness of visions and dreams deferred, of broken promises and misspent energies—of all the things I, and we, had done and left undone—but also an awareness that all of it flowed into a mighty river of love that refuses to give up on us. I didn't hear any voices, no audible words, but the way I would now describe it is this: it was as if God had gotten in my face to say, "OK, I know all that, but now it's time to *stop nibbling!*"

Graced Practice in Congregational Life

It seemed to me that this epiphany, this call to stop nibbling, addressed not only my own circumstances but the life of my congregation, for one of the serious challenges faced by churches engaged in urban ministry is fragmentation of energy (mental, spiritual, and physical). This fragmentation impedes growth into the holistic life prescribed by the Great Commandment. As I mentioned in the introduction, urban congregations devote time, energy, and attention to all the basic demands of church life such as budgets, building and maintenance, personnel issues, and the worship, education, and nurture of the its members. But they also can find themselves grappling with challenging issues endemic to city life: homelessness, scarcity of living wage jobs, racism, mental illness, crime, and educational and economic disparities. Any one of these issues could completely absorb a congregation's time and energy, and achieving a measure of balance is challenging. Thus, upon returning to Washington, D.C., after my time in Colorado, I proposed to the leadership of the New York Avenue Presbyterian Church (the session in Presbyterian polity) that we begin a new initiative: that of nurturing in our own lives and in the life of the congregation as a whole a disciplined balance of heart, mind, and will in our service to God and neighbor—disciplined integration of our spiritual, mental, and physical energies in our collective endeavors of worship, education, and activism. It was my hope that this initiative would enable the leadership to facilitate for the congregation as a whole a more balanced, holistic sense of ministry as defined in the Great Commandment entrusted to us by Jesus.

Failure to address intentionally and directly the problem of fragmentation can result in burnout, loss of energy, loss of purpose, and a loss of a sense for the whole—in short, loss of vision and diminution of the mission with which we are entrusted. A certain loss of vision and fragmentation in overall mission was evident in several of our ministries at New York Avenue Presbyterian Church. For example, we have been engaged in an ongoing ministry on Sunday morning during which hospitality (food and fellowship) is extended to more than one hundred homeless people in our neighborhood. After our homeless ministry ends downstairs (in what is known as our Radcliffe Room Ministry), corporate worship begins in our sanctuary upstairs. Some of our homeless friends join us in worship (indeed, some are members of the church), but many folk (members and homeless friends alike) lack a clear sense of the connection between the ministry of hospitality that goes on downstairs and the worship that goes on upstairs. A vital connection needed to be made between these two dynamic aspects of our church life if we were to live more deeply into the commandment to love God and neighbors as ourselves.

Urban ministry demands a willingness to live and work in places of ambiguity between the real and the ideal—in what I have termed the "trenches of ministry." It takes revolutionary patience to live amid tensions between the "world as it is" and the "world as it should be" and, by the grace of God, to nudge it slowly from one point to the other. So, in the initiative that I proposed to the leadership of the church, I urged us to tackle the challenge of integrating heart, mind, and will in all our ministries—a balance that is essential to ministry when homelessness, unemployment or underemployment, consumer indebtedness, and dysfunctional civil politics collide with the everyday lives of parishioners who are striving to live faithfully as disciples of Jesus Christ amid their own fear, anger, and incessant meandering.

The model for this proposal was the three-legged stool of which I have spoken at several points throughout this volume—a stool with a stabilizing post in the middle, connecting the three legs that have become my template for ministry: one leg solidly grounded in the life of the mind (theology, ethics, philosophy, and current affairs); a second leg grounded in the life of the will (as it finds expression in social activism and life in the world); and a third leg grounded in the life of the heart (the experiences of communal worship and the contemplative). In my view, the post in the middle of the stool, stabilizing the legs, represents the integration of heart, mind, and will as it lives into the Great Commandment.

I initially asked for and received permission from our governing board to form an ad hoc committee of ruling elders to devise a plan for the implementation of a "disciplined intention" to balance the ministry of heart, mind, and will (worship, education, and activism) in our corporate life. The overall intent of the plan was to covenant with the session, and eventually with the other governing boards of the church (deacons and trustees) as well, to attend to the holistic demands of the Great Commandment in all our life and work together. I also asked for and received a commitment from ministerial staff members of NYAPC to work toward the same goal. Thankfully, it was an initiative that both the session and staff also recognized and embraced as their own.

It was my sincere hope that intentional engagement with the vision of the Great Commandment—one that urges integration of heart, mind, and will, or of worship, education and activism—would generate new spiritual vitality for the leadership of The New York Avenue Presbyterian Church (myself included) and for all the ministries within the congregation that they oversee. I was also hopeful that it would generate new visions for the session as a board as it contemplated the future of our ministry and eventually move us toward a long-range vision for our congregation. Finally, I was hopeful that our experience might assist and encourage other urban parishes struggling with issues of fragmentation.

We are still in the midst of living into this initiative. So how is it going? What has happened so far? The session began by covering the waterfront of spiritual practice using Marjorie Thompson's *Soul Feast: An Invitation to the Christian Spiritual Life* as a baseline for our work. It seemed to us to be an important place to start because most of our folk have highly developed minds and wills—that is, our minds and our wills have had a great deal of exercise, because we work hard at the educational task of understanding the Christian faith, and we actively engage our faith in a range of social ministries in our community. But our hearts tend to be underdeveloped. *Soul Feast* offers a very fine introduction to the varied dimensions of basic spiritual practices, such as the spiritual reading of Scripture (*lectio divina*), varied kinds of prayer practices, fasting, self-examination, worship, spiritual direction, hospitality, and developing a rule of faith. After we read through the book, surveying the landscape, we then decided to slow down and digest what we had read. Following the advice of an educator among our leadership, we reread and discussed one chapter at a time at every monthly session meeting and engaged together in some of the spiritual practices discussed in the book. Among the varied practices we engaged as a group were spiritual reading of Scripture, centering prayer, and the prayer of daily examination. Moreover, each elder (that is, each member of the session) was encouraged to participate in the solitude retreats that are part of our church calendar.

These solitude retreats are offered on a regular basis at the New York Avenue Presbyterian Church. An urban church is typically busy and noisy, feverishly so. But three to four times a year (usually on a Saturday), The New York Avenue Church shuts down its business and dedicates the building to the contemplative arts. Participants find a variety of contemplative practices available to choose from. They can listen to Gregorian chants in a sanctuary darkened for prayer or meditate on the stained glass windows, practicing *lectio divina* with Scripture appropriate to each window. Different rooms within the church building are dedicated to labyrinth walking, spiritual conversation, meditative yoga, and journaling. The solitude retreats remind members of the congregation as well as our city neighbors (we advertise the retreats on billboards on the sidewalks) that space is needed amid frenetic schedules for the contemplation of the transcendent One in whom we live and move and have our being.

Solitude retreats are also critical to my own spiritual journey as a pastor. Early in my ministry, in my first solo pastorate in Baltimore, there came a point at which I "hit the wall." I was on the verge of burning out. Ministry had become a dry desert, as I felt overwhelmed by the endless needs in the church and the city and had decreasing energy to engage them. The community organizing ventures were inspiring, and the church was working with great integrity and passion to address the needs of the city as well as the needs of its members. But there was only one of me, and my well was running dry. The wick of an oil-burning lamp will drain just about every drop of oil out of the lamp until it finally sputters out, and my lamp was sputtering! So along with two clergy friends I enrolled in a course on spiritual direction with the Oasis Ministries in Camp Hill, Pennsylvania. Thus for two years I dined on a smorgasbord of arts required for spiritual direction and therein discovered my own real need to attend to the contemplative. I have since become a devotee of the Spiritual Exercises of St. Ignatius in an adapted Protestant/Reformed format. I furthered my education in the Ignatian Exercises with the help of the Retreat Directors Workshop and the Communal Discernment Workshop at Loyola House of Guelph, Ontario, Canada. It is not an exaggeration to say that these exercises have saved my life and renewed my ministry, providing new directions for me and my ministry. Indeed, I'm quite certain that these contemplative arts are the reason I am still engaged in ministry.

But I've also learned that one size doesn't fit all people. Our solitude retreats provide a range of contemplative offerings, but even these retreats are not suited for everyone. I have also had to acknowledge that the Spiritual Exercises of St. Ignatius, which have become such a rich part of my own contemplative practice, are not a good fit for everyone. Thus in my work with the session, the most pressing question was how to accommodate diverse spiritual aptitudes and preferences while addressing the critical need for some manner of contemplative space.

The need to address in a disciplined manner the contemplative dimension of the life of faith was at the heart of the epiphany I experienced at the junction of the two streams in the Rocky Mountain National Park—the call to "stop nibbling." I am now more convinced than ever that contemplative space—in other words, the "conscious desire to enter more deeply into the divine Eros that flows through all things"[7]—is an essential aspect of the Christian life and something every believer needs to attend to in some way, shape, or form. We all need encouragement to stop nibbling! Indeed, I have become downright "evangelical" in my zeal to help people create space in their lives for the transformation of heart, mind, and will so that they can grow more fully into the love of God, neighbor, and self. The very practical question, however, is how to go about this.

As I sought an answer to this question, I was compelled by the final chapter of *Soul Feast*, in which Marjorie Thompson discusses the importance of developing a "rule of life":

> A rule of life is a pattern of spiritual disciplines that provide structure and direction for growth in holiness. When we speak of patterns in our life, we mean attitudes, behaviors, or elements that are routine, repeated, regular. . . . A rule of life is not meant to be restrictive, although it certainly asks for genuine commitment. It is meant to help us establish a rhythm of daily living, a basic order within which new freedoms can grow.[8]

What we were in need of was something spiritual and religious, something contemplative and disciplined that would accommodate each person's aptitude for what that might look like in their own life. I was also interested in finding a discipline that we, as a session, could engage together while at the same time allowing room for each to define a particular path. I was hoping that each person would find a fitting formative practice they could mold to their own schedule and personality. I was also hoping that their practice would be infectious, bearing not only on their life together as a leadership group but on the whole church.

The Covenant

After much conversation and practice, the governing board finally agreed on a covenant that we would embrace for a year, with renewal possible in the following year. The covenant encompassed the three legs of the stool; heart, mind, and will. First, we agreed to daily engagement with an individual prayer practice between our monthly meetings (a practice of the heart).

We allowed for some breadth in this practice while offering resources each month that included praying with specified Scriptures using the *lectio divina* style of meditation and meditative readings from spiritual masters. We also covenanted to pray on a regular basis for one another and members of the congregation. Second, we covenanted to read a chapter of a book on ministry each month (a practice of the mind). The pastors provided several reading suggestions but especially identified books on hospitality. Third, each member of the session agreed to conduct one relational meeting each month with a member of the congregation or someone related to our ministry (a practice of the will and an exercise of power with others). To prepare them for this last practice, I conducted relational meeting training so that it was clear that these meetings were not about tasks but about telling stories: they could be faith stories; stories about family, friends, vocation, mentors; stories of joys, pain, passion, anger, injustice, healing, liberation, and redemption. Finally, we agreed to spend the first thirty minutes of our monthly session meetings in small groups, sharing from our experience of these commitments. The small group meetings would be focused on the following questions: Where are you spiritually? What are you learning from your reading or the relational meetings you have done? What bearing do these things have on your work as an elder?

As the leadership dove into this new venture, what happened, I suppose, was predictable but also unpredictable—like the movement of the Spirit. Some took to the covenant like fish to water. They were intentional about relational meetings, reading, and prayer. Others found engagement with intentional contemplative practices more challenging. One of our leaders characterized our efforts to embrace these practices as a series of "baby steps." If so, that is fine with me. I'd rather have the baby attempting to walk than still in the crib.

In terms of my own impressions, I discerned a palpable change in the ethos of our meetings. The thirty minutes we spent discussing our spiritual practice not only held people accountable for the practice but also set a tone for our meetings. There is something truly inspiring about communal conversation in light of Jesus' promise that "where two or three are gathered in my name, I am there among them" (Matt. 18:20). I was thrilled when, in the midst of discussing a difficult decision that we had to make, someone stopped us and said, "I think this is something we should pray about." I thought to myself: Yes!—because she didn't offer that suggestion as an afterthought but rather as an essential part of faithful decision-making. Something had changed.

My hope and intent for our graced practice is that we will continue to grow in our practice of what I term as "cruciform spirituality." This entails

recognizing our brokenness and our yearning for God; it also entails discerning the places where God is bringing life and where there is covenant community. The central paradox of our faith is that the gifts to serve emerge from the
wounds—from the crosses—of our lives, for the divine love is seeking us out
in the midst of our fear, our anger, and our incessant meandering, setting us
free from them and empowering us to love. Resurrection emerges from such
places, enabling us to grow more fully into love of God, neighbor, and self.

Practicum

While the questions for reflection that follow may be engaged by individual
readers, they might also be engaged collectively by the leadership body of
your congregation. For example, you could ask your governing board to read
this chapter and then, in a special meeting or series of meetings, discuss the
following questions:

> What strikes you most about the discussion of "the contemplative" in
> this chapter? What questions does it raise for you?
> Does the image of "nibbling" speak to your life and that of your con-
> gregation? If so, how? If not, why not? Be as specific as possible,
> keeping in mind the aspirations of the Great Commandment. In what
> sense could expressions of "nibbling" be said to represent the reality
> of crucifixion in our lives? How might it foster our complicity in the
> reality of crucifixions all around us?
> Does Luke's spiritual topography speak to your own spiritual state and
> that of your congregation? Are realities of fear, anger, or incessant
> meandering obstacles in your practice of the Christian life? If so, how?
> What does the incarnation of God in Christ mean to you? Reflect on
> the statement that "incarnation is about God coming close, becoming
> flesh, fully experiencing our utter fear, rage, and meandering."
> What do you think of the description of "the contemplative" in this chap-
> ter as space where we can find release from fear, rage, and anxious
> meandering—and discover our yearning for God and God's yearning
> for us? Do you find this appealing, challenging, or important? Why,
> or why not? What role does "the contemplative" play in your own life
> of faith and that of your congregation?
> Do fragmentation, burnout, and fatigue manifest themselves in the life
> and ministry of your congregation? And do they contribute to loss of
> energy and focus? Why or why not? Do your ministries intention-
> ally seek to integrate the love of God and love of neighbor enjoined
> upon us by the Great Commandment? Do your ministries effectively

engage the mind, the heart, and the will? That is, are educational, contemplative, and activist practice integrated in the life of your congregation? Which aspects receive greater (or lesser) energy and attention? Do you think disciplined, intentional contemplative practices of the sort discussed in this chapter can play a contagious role within the life and ministry of your congregation? Why or why not?

Share your reaction to the notion of "cruciform spirituality" or the recognition of our brokenness and discerning the places where God is bringing life, thus enabling us to grow more fully into love of God, neighbor, and self.

Consider again Marjorie Thompson's description of the rule of faith:

A rule of life is a pattern of spiritual disciplines that provide structure and direction for growth in holiness. When we speak of patterns in our life, we mean attitudes, behaviors, or elements that are routine, repeated, regular . . . . A rule of life is not meant to be restrictive, although it certainly asks for genuine commitment. It is meant to help us establish a rhythm of daily living, a basic order within which new freedoms can grow.[9]

As an individual and as a group, engage the question: What might a rule of faith look like for us?

After engaging these questions, I invite you to slow down. If your congregation is like mine, the mind and the will may be more developed than the heart. Thus, I suggest that you read Marjorie Thompson's *Soul Feast* chapter by chapter, using the group study guide in the back of the book and practicing the varied disciplines described. After a period of three or four months, consider whether your group might be willing to articulate a covenant that would deepen your practice of the contemplative. Any covenant should be both structured and flexible—structured enough to provide guidance but flexible enough to allow each participant to discern spiritual practices that suit him or her best. Finally, I strongly urge you to consider including an activist component in this covenant, such as the relational meeting. The benefit of a relational meeting component is that it will include the larger community in the purview of the group's practice.

Chapter 5

Teaching Moments

Doing Theology in the Local Parish

Not long ago during a worship service at The New York Avenue Presbyterian Church, when the time came for the sharing of concerns and announcements, I was on the verge of alerting the congregation to an upcoming event related to jobs sponsored by the Washington Interfaith Network when my ministry colleague, Linda Lader, passed me a note. I was a bit taken aback, because the note suggested that I provide a theological rationale for making this pitch. At first I bristled! I thought to myself, I have done so much preaching and teaching on the subject of the church in public life, and my congregants are engaged in such a range of social ministries that I am quite sure they get it! But then I realized that Linda was right. In our time and place, we must clearly articulate theological reasons for engagement with the world and should not presume it is unnecessary to do. It was a teaching moment for me. Doug Ottati is spot-on when he claims that many socially engaged Christians "appear to know almost intuitively where they stand on important issues of the day. . . . Too often, however they seem unable to give strong theological reasons for the stand they take. Indeed, some liberal Protestants appear to regard theological reflection as only an ancillary head trip that detracts from the real business at hand."[1] Throughout this book, I have attempted to do just what Ottati suggests: to provide theological grounding for the life and work of the urban church. We can never say too much about this. We can always do more to help socially engaged Christians articulate their faith, and in this chapter I aim to underscore the importance of this task.

In the previous four chapters, we have considered some basic tools that can help us live into the Great Commandment in our practice of ministry, both within the church and in the community around us. In the opening chapter, we explored a theological framework for the church's engagement in the world using four prepositions: the church is *in, with, against,* and *for* the world. In the second and third chapters, we examined two community-organizing tools—the relational meeting and listening sessions—as theologically apt resources for parish life. In the fourth chapter, we considered the importance of disciplined integration of heart, mind, and will as a means by which to live more fully into the Great Commandment. As we considered these practices within the life of the church, several questions arose that I have addressed briefly but now need further attention. I want to highlight four questions in particular that have evoked significant teaching moments in my life as a pastor and in the life of the congregation—moments in which I have had to think deeply about my own faith and my assumptions about the church in the world and to help others do the same.

The first is the question of Christ and culture. Many simply assume that cultural tools (such as community organizing, the best management practices of the business community, or therapeutic wisdom) are fair game for use in the church. I address this assumption in the first section of this chapter. The second question concerns the notion of "self-interest." In community organizing, as in politics, it is assumed that one organizes around people's self-interest. For example, in the opening chapter, I referred to this term in connection with the organization of folk in the church neighborhood on the occasion of the closing of the local grocery store. Yet what does it mean for Christians to speak of "self-interest" when our model for Christian living is the self-giving love of God in Christ? In the second section of this chapter, I articulate a Christian understanding of self-interest.

These two questions and the teaching moments they have evoked have raised other questions. If Christian faith is not insular to the life of the church but has significant ramifications for our life in the world, then what do traditional beliefs, such as those expressed in the Apostles' Creed, have to do with urban life? And what does Christian witness look like in pluralistic settings like Washington, D.C., and other urban areas where devotees of all the world's religions reside? These last two questions, regarding tradition and religious pluralism, also provide opportunities for urban Christians and will be addressed in the final two sections of this chapter.

Christ and Culture

In some circles in which I move, community-organizing tools play an important role in energizing and mobilizing congregations for urban and social ministry, as they have in my own ministry. In other circles, best business and management practices from the corporate world are revered as antidotes to ecclesial malaise. In still others, therapeutic wisdom is regarded as the magic potion for the practice of ministry. For example, in the preface to the 2011 edition of Edwin Friedman's much-read book *Generation to Generation*, an application of family systems therapy to congregational settings, a devotee of Freidman stated, "Rabbi Jesus saved my soul, but Rabbi Friedman saved my ass."[2] It is of course the better part of wisdom to avail ourselves of tools, strategies, and skills that we can glean from other arenas of human cultural endeavor—any resources that will enhance our practice of ministry. But the question remains: Can they ever be described as fundamental or essential to the renewal of the church? This is the "Christ and culture" question, as H. Richard Niebuhr's classic study put it, and wrestling with it has played an increasingly important role in my own theological reflection and in my preaching, teaching, and conversation with members of my congregation.

In varied ecclesial contexts, people grasp for techniques or best practices from varied cultural contexts as resources for ministry. Some take it for granted that these resources are fair game for use in the church while others raise questions about the church's use of them. I find myself on both sides of this debate. On the one hand, I want to affirm engagement with such practices; but on the other hand I am uncomfortable when we use cultural resources uncritically and without theological reflection—when we regard such resources as synonymous with the gospel itself or as essential tools for the renewal of ministry. Let me share some thoughts on both sides of this question in hopes that it may evoke reflection and perhaps a teaching moment for you, too.

There is something to be said for engagement with best cultural practices. Noted biblical scholar Walter Wink draws a direct correlation between the nonviolent strategies of community organizing and those taught by Jesus. Wink discusses Jesus' challenging instructions to his disciples in the Sermon on the Mount to turn the other cheek and walk the extra mile, emphasizing that Jesus is not recommending passivity but rather nonviolent resistance to insulting and demeaning practices. He notes, for example, that Roman military law allowed a soldier to conscript a citizen of an occupied country to carry his pack for one mile—but one mile only. Thus, to carry a soldier's pack an extra mile would place him in violation of the law, thereby discomfiting him. Moreover, by walking the extra mile, one seizes the initiative and thus takes back the power of choice. Wink then amplifies these insights by drawing a comparison between Jesus and Saul Alinsky, the renowned community organizer and founder of the Industrial Areas Foundation (IAF, of which WIN, the Washington Interfaith Network, is an affiliate): "Jesus, like Alinsky, recommended using your experience of being belittled, insulted, or dispossessed in such a way as to seize the initiative from the oppressor, who finds reactions like going the second mile totally outside his experience. This forces him to take your power seriously and perhaps to recognize your humanity." [3]

The folklore of the IAF is replete with such stories. In BUILD (the IAF affiliate in Baltimore), one such celebrated story was of an initiative taken when a bank manager refused to meet with representatives from the community who wanted to discuss the bank's practice of redlining (that is, denying) loans to people living in a poor neighborhood. BUILD members organized the neighborhood, and on a designated day a huge crowd (including a large number of church people) showed up to open bank accounts—with rolls upon rolls of pennies. The lines were so long and the process of counting thousands upon thousands of pennies so slow that they managed to completely tie up business. His business stymied, the exasperated bank manager finally agreed to meet with them. The meeting was productive, and eventually the bank's practice of redlining came to an end. I suspect Jesus would have been mighty proud of the creative initiative of those folk in Baltimore.

There is important wisdom to be gained for ministry as we engage insights and practices gleaned from culture—whether from community organizers like Saul Alinsky, civil rights leaders like Gandhi, business gurus, or therapeutic sages like Edwin Friedman. Those familiar with H. Richard Niebuhr's classic "Christ and culture" typologies of the Christian's relationship to culture will recognize this as the "Christ of culture" model, wherein Christ is identified with the best of cultural practices. As Niebuhr points out, Jesus himself "found some wise people of his day nearer to the kingdom of God than others." [4] The "Christ of culture" model is appealing because it makes it possible for us to find common ground with non-Christians in working for the common good.

Indeed, the Christ of culture model is one that resonates with me in many respects. But the moment I make this confession, the Calvinist within me begins to squirm a bit, prompting theological reflection, because one thing about which Calvinists are certain is that our best efforts are shot through with sin. For the Calvinist, sin is so pervasive that we would not even see it were it not for the grace of God. So as much as I admire and embrace the Christ of culture (and thus the best practices of culture), engagement with them must be critically informed by my faith in the crucified and risen Christ, which always begins with truly fundamental questions—cruciform questions of suspicion and grace. Suspicion asks the question, Who or what is being crucified? The lens of grace asks the question, Where is God bringing justice, reconciliation, life, and resurrection out of the death-tending ways of the world? These fundamental questions are more likely to emerge, I think, in what Niebuhr refers to as the "Christ transforming culture" version of the Christian faith, and, in my view, more adequately reflect the Christian's primary posture in the world. This posture is reflected in the four prepositions we engaged in chapter 1 to explicate the church's relationship to the world: The church is *in* the world, never giving up on God's good creation; *with* the world, confessing our common faults and sins; and *against* the world, bearing prophetic witness to God's intentions for human life and the whole creation. The church is also, finally, *for* the world because the church is a community of hope.

The chief problem that Niebuhr identifies with the "Christ *of* culture" version of Christianity is that it tends to stumble on the offense of the cross of Christ,[5] for the cross exposes the sins pervading the world even in the best of human achievement. However, the cross also provides an instructive lens for the use of cultural wisdom. When we utilize the lens of the cruciform faith, the following criterion emerges: worldly wisdom is useful when it aids us in discerning the places where God is bringing justice, reconciliation, and life out of brokenness. In other words, worldly wisdom can be a valuable resource but only as it is placed in the service of cruciform faith. Indeed, in the first three chapters of this book, I suggested that community organizing tools (such as the relational meeting and the listening campaign) can be very useful in facilitating collective discernment of the Easter dynamics of dying and rising in our midst or ways in which we might live more fully into the Great Commandment as we engage in the practice of ministry.

In sum, identification of Jesus with the wisdom and best practices of human culture can be instructive, even inspiring; but for Christians, they are not the primary lens through which ministry is engaged and renewed—they are decidedly secondary. The foundation of Christian vision, and the criterion for use of cultural wisdom, is the crucified and risen Christ who refocuses our hearts, minds, and wills on the depth of our own sins and the sins of the world and then redirects us toward loving God and neighbor and participation in God's work of mending the creation.

The next chapter illustrates the importance of this criterion, as I describe how four churches within the WIN organization came to recognize that we had to address the issue of racism and poverty in Washington, D.C. We did not reach this point primarily via the tools of community organizing but rather through the lens of the cross of America's original sins: racism and slavery. Yet in coming together to reflect on racism, we discovered grace and power for ministry in our community and thus returned to our work of organizing for jobs, housing, and an end to homelessness with renewed passion and commitment.

Self-Interest

Throughout my engagement in urban ministry with community-organizing affiliations and practices, I have found myself ruminating on the concept of "self-interest"—a key concept in community organizing, as in politics, for it is assumed that one organizes around people's self-interest. Addressing questions related to this basic concept—both my own and those of others—has provided another teaching moment requiring theological reflection. In chapter 1, I shared a story about a neighborhood grocery store and described how a diverse community in Baltimore organized around their respective self-interest in it. I spoke of how "we" and "them" became "us" over the course of our organizing. The use of the term "self-interest" in connection with ventures such as this one is seldom analyzed within a Christian theological framework, but it needs to be. Christians, after all, proclaim the self-giving love of Jesus Christ, so how can they also be guided by self-interest? Can these concepts exist in the same theological universe? I touched on this question in chapter 1:

> One of the chief polarities recognized by organizations such as BUILD, founded on the principles of the Industrial Areas Foundation (IAF), is the tension between "the world as it is" and "the world as it should be." In "the world as it is," self-interest is the prime motivator for survival and leads to individualism and selfish behavior. The IAF, however, teaches that self-interest can actually be a relation-building, world-affirming motivation—it can move us toward the "world as it should be." The root etymology of the word "interest" is a combination of two Latin terms: *inter*, which can be translated "between" or "among," and *esse*, which can be translated "to be." Therefore, self-interest can mean something like "self interrelated to one's essence." What this suggests is that our interest is not trapped inside us but also resides within our relations with others. Another way of putting the matter is that our essential selves are found in covenant relations to others and God.
>
> Some may question any notion of "self-interest" as a basis for relating to God and others. However, as Sondra Wheeler helpfully observes, "the ultimate moral ideal to which theologians like Augustine point is not really the suppression of self-love in favor of love for others. It is instead a vision of love rightly ordered, with the love of God being both the source and limit of all proper loves for created things. Only those who love God above all else can love God's creatures, including themselves, as they should." Self-interest thus has everything to do with being in the world in relation to others and to God; it has everything to do with our covenant life before the sovereign God of creation. So when the BUILD churches in Baltimore

entered into relationship with the residents who lived around that closed grocery store, it was not out of charity, or even liberal activism. We got involved because it was essential to our being, for to live fully and abundantly is to live with and for others and with God, or to put it another way, to live a full covenant life before the sovereign God of creation.[6]

As I introduced the concept of self-interest in that earlier chapter, I hoped not only to present a fundamental principle of IAF organizing but also to place it within the theological framework of creation, fall, and redemption—the full sweep of the Christian story. More needs to be said about that so that church folk will have a theologically informed grasp of this principle as they engage it. So what might "self-interest" look like from a consciously Christian perspective? However we use the term—whether as a synonym for selfish behavior or for more enlightened (relation-building) behavior—it is crucial for our understanding of others and ourselves. The relational meeting is a tool that helps us deeply know one another; relational meetings reveal our core motivations. The goal of such a meeting is to know something of the *essence* of others, their guiding *self-interests*.

Awareness of self-interest is also crucial to our understanding of ourselves, because Christians are also motivated by it—in both selfish and enlightened senses of the word. It manifests itself in our lives in both appropriate and damaging ways. Christians have appropriate self-interest in living out of our essential relation to God, others, and self—in learning to love God, others, and self in ways that show forth the image of God in which we were made and thereby to contribute to the divine purpose. Yet Christians are also realistic about the fact that as frail children of dust, our deepest essence (as creatures created in the image of God) is crusted over with anxious, fearful, and addictive striving that warps us and keeps us from the fullness of life that God intends for us. Anxiety, as many theologians have noted, is not sin, but the precondition of sin. As anxiety about life and death, meaning and purpose, grasp us at our core, self-interest can become selfish, distorting, and deforming. The traditional word we use for this deformation is sin. So the question is, How does one move from deformation toward reformation of the self in relation to God and others so that we might live more fully into the Great Commandment? While I have addressed this question in the preceding chapters, in what follows I want to add another angle of vision to the discussion. I want us to consider how a "Christian transformation of self-interest" can empower us for our work in the world.

As I have reflected on the transformation of self-interest—on what it means to be guided by self-interest in ways that further our human vocation of reflecting the image of God and living fully into the Great Commandment—I have found myself returning time and again to a scene in Walker Percy's novel *The Second Coming*. The central character of the story, Will Barrett, has been having blackout spells accompanied by dark thoughts about his life even though he seemingly has it all—friends, family, wealth. But one day when he returns home after playing golf, while sitting in his driveway with the car door open, he has a revelation. His cat is sitting in the driveway sunning himself, and Will Barrett suddenly realizes what had gone wrong in his universe. He thinks, "There was the cat. Sitting there in the sun with its needs satisfied, for whom one place was the same as any other as long as it was sunny. . . . The cat was exactly a hundred percent cat, no more, no less. As for Will Barrett, as for people nowadays, they were never one hundred percent themselves. They occupied their place uneasily. . . . All too often these days they were two percent themselves, specters who hardly occupied a place at all."[7] Will Barrett then concludes his diagnosis with this revelatory question: "How can the great suck of self ever hope to be a fat cat dozing in the sun?"[8] In a similar vein, Thomas Merton once wrote: "A tree gives glory to God by being a tree."[9] In other words, the tree is giving glory to God simply by living out God's intentions for it. And if that is true, then Will Barrett's question remains most relevant: How can the great suck of self ever hope to be a tree or a fat cat sitting in the sun? How can we learn to live out God's intentions for our lives?

"The great suck of self," as I interpret it, represents self-interest in its negative manifestations—what we would recognize as egocentrism or distorting and deforming expressions of self-interest. Theologian Wendy Farley points out that egocentrism can manifest itself either as pride or as self-denigration, because both entail an absorption with oneself. I would add that either form of self-absorption is a kind of crucifixion, for in each case we experience ourselves as cut off, separated, exiled from the rightly ordered love we need.[10]

So if our core problem is crucifying self-absorption that disfigures our lives—whether it is the result of pride or self-denigration or some other wound—how do we move from deformed to enlightened self-interest? How can self-interest be transmuted from self-absorption to rightly ordered love of God, others, and self? I would contend that we are liberated from the grasp of "the great suck of self" only in authentic encounter with God and with neighbors who draw us out of ourselves and that movement out of the grave of self-absorption can be instigated in a variety of ways. Service with and for others, for example, is one means by which self-interest is transformed in life-affirming ways. Thus in the story shared in the first chapter, shared self-interest in a grocery store led to joint service to the community in which strangers became friends. Careful listening to God and to others can also be means by which we are drawn out of ourselves. Contemplative disciplines facilitate attention to God, and practices such as the relational meeting or listening sessions can facilitate emergence from self-absorption. Attentive, holy listening to both God and neighbors can release us from self-absorption, expand our vision, and help us discern where God is bringing life out of death and summoning us to endeavors that give expression to rightly ordered love.

Interestingly, such catalysts for movement out of graves of self-absorption appear in close proximity to the Great Commandment in the Gospel of Luke's presentation of it (Luke 10:25–28). Indeed, the Great Commandment is followed by three back-to-back episodes that elaborate upon it: a story about a good Samaritan in 10:29–37 (that prompts reflection on love of and service to neighbor), the story of Mary and Martha in 10:38–42 (that prompts reflection on love of and attentiveness to God in Christ), and Jesus' instruction on prayer in 11:1–13 (which is a means by which we listen to God and discern the divine intention for our lives). All three of these episodes feature means by which we may experience regenerative encounters with God or neighbors and thereby grow out of self-absorption and more fully into the dual love prescribed by the Great Commandment.

One of these means of encountering another—the "service" or love of neighbor exemplified by the good Samaritan—may need a further word of explication, because the concept of "service" is easily misunderstood. Why? In my experience, there is a tricky downside to service, given the thin line between humble service and humiliation. Indeed, many in our world experience labor in the "service industry" as a humiliating occupation. Service workers occupy the lowest rung on the economic ladder and testify that they often feel demeaned and devalued. Others, whose primary labor is in service to their families and takes the form of "housework," also witness to a sense that their labor is demeaned and devalued. This raises the question of whether it is possible to restore "service" to its rightful place as a means of glorifying God and as a means by which we experience the transformation of self-interest as a life-giving reality.

Wendy Farley provides an interfaith perspective worth sharing, as it addresses this dilemma. She calls attention to a fascinating correspondence between the Buddhist notion of "*vajra* pride" and the Christian notion of being "in Christ." *Vajra* literally means "lightning bolt," and in Tibetan Buddhism it denotes a severing (as a knife severs) of the self from self-absorption so that one is liberated or freed for compassion and service. And, most important, it denotes a power to serve that is not bound by either selfishness or humiliation. Farley puts it this way:

Vajra pride is an image, borrowed from another language and culture, for an order of existence that is not governed by the duality of selfishness and humiliation. It is an image for the joy that comes as we find ways to unhook ourselves from the pathologies of egocentrism . . . . It reminds us of the excessive modesty of our self-understanding. "Who am I to be compassionate or wise? Who am I to shine like the sun?" Who are you that you do not recognize who you are? Who are you that you defraud yourself of your intimacy with Christ, with nature, with beauty, with other people? Who are you that you are sick and exhausted from holding back your stupendous power to love and feel and live? . . . We are God-bearers. As our trust in this reality becomes more stable, we will become less afraid. As we discover practices that help us live into this reality, we dismantle the polarity that bounces us between our self-inflation and self-hatred, our addictions and our terror.[11]

Farley also contends that *vajra* pride corresponds to Paul's notion that "it is no longer I who live, but it is Christ who lives in me" (Gal. 2:20).[12] In Galatians, Paul tells us that when we exist "in Christ," the flesh (Paul's word for self-absorption) is "crucified." As a result, we are freed to live life in the power of the Spirit—a life of love, joy, patience, faithfulness, and generosity (Gal. 5:22–25). Life that is lived in the power of the Spirit entails Christ-empowered service that gives glory to God.

The Christian's service is patterned on the life of Jesus himself, and one final perspective may be helpful as we ponder what this means for our own service in his name. As we are reminded every Maundy Thursday, Jesus said, "If I, your Lord and Teacher, have washed your feet, you also ought to wash one another's feet. For I have set you an example, that you also should do as I have done to you" (John 13:14–15). In her astute commentary on Jesus' washing of his disciples' feet in John's Gospel, Sandra Schneiders draws attention to an intriguing aspect of this act and to what it suggests about the distinctive nature of the service that characterizes the Christian life. She observes that we encounter three very different models of serving in our everyday experience, and thus it is important to be clear about the model in view here. "In the first model service denotes what one person (the server) must do for another (the served) because of some right or power that the latter is understood to possess." As she notes, this kind of service arises from "a fundamental condition of inequality between two persons" and is thus the kind of service that a slave renders to a master, that the poor render to the rich, or that women in a patriarchal society render to men. In the second model, "service denotes what the server does freely for the served because of some need perceived in the latter that the former has the power to meet." It is in this sense that parents serve their children, professionals serve their clients, the rich serve the poor, and the strong serve the weak. However, in this model too, the basis of the service is inequality. The third, quite different model of service is that of friendship, "the one human relationship based on equality." In friendship, Schneiders notes, *the good of each is truly the other's good and so, in seeking the good of the friend, one's own good is achieved*." It is this friendship model of service that characterizes Jesus' service to his disciples and their service to others that follows his lead. In fact, Jesus articulates this explicitly, describing his self-gift as an act of friendship: "I do not call you servants any longer . . . I have called you friends" (15:15).[13]

This kind of service and friendship—in which "the good of each is truly the other's good and so, in seeking the good of the friend, one's own good is achieved"—is a manifestation of "self-interest" in the very best sense of the word. It is truly "self interrelated to one's essence," as our attention to etymology suggested, in the sense that our interest is not trapped inside us but resides within our relations with others. Our essential selves are found in covenant relations to others and God. This is what I had in mind in my initial description of self-interest in chapter 1 when I suggested that we enter into relationship with others not out of charity, or even liberal activism, but rather because it is essential to our being. We enter into relationship with others in order to live fully and abundantly, out of the love defined in the Great Commandment: love of God and of neighbor as self.

In sum, self-interest is not a concept alien to Christian theological reflection. One way or another, we will find ourselves motivated by self-interest. As deforming manifestations of self-interest in our lives are exposed and transformed through service and attentive, holy listening to God and to others, by God's grace we are liberated from lives of self-absorption and enter into the fulfilling experience of loving God, neighbor, and self in ways that bear witness to our true identity as God's own people who are formed in the divine image. As such, we are shaped for joyful service in the world patterned on Jesus' example that seeks the good of others as our own good. Like the tree that gives glory to God by being a tree, we give glory to God by living out of our essential nature. Released from "the great suck of self," we can be fat cats basking in the sun.

Engaging the Christian Tradition

I trust that it is clear that I do not shy away from explicating Christian theology in any aspect of my ministry and from inviting theological reflection and conversation as a crucial resource for discerning what God is calling us to be and do. Why? On the one hand, theology does not fulfill its purpose until it is placed in the service of explicating and illuminating the practices of church and our life in the world. On the other hand, the practices of the church and our life in the world do not fulfill their purpose until they are integrated into and placed in service of our relationship to God. At its best, theology helps us with these tasks. At its worst, theology is arcane and irrelevant. I believe that theology is profoundly relevant, indeed essential, to the life of discipleship and to the church's corporate life and mission in the world, and one of my chief responsibilities as a pastor and Christian educator is to facilitate engagement with the rich resources of the Christian theological tradition. In this section, I make the case that doing theology in the church is essential in that it helps people make sense of the life of the church. I will do so by tackling what is sometimes viewed as one of the church's most arcane artifacts: the Apostles' Creed.

On occasion, I have taken leave of lectionary-based preaching in order to address the Apostles' Creed and its relevance for contemporary urban life. I have done so in both urban parishes I have served, in Baltimore and Washington, frankly because some members within each congregation made no secret of their longstanding feud with it; some declared it enigmatic, and others found it downright offensive. Indeed, both congregations had stopped using it in worship, even though the Presbyterian *Book of Order*—part 2 of the constitution of the PC(USA)—mandates its use in the liturgy of baptism. So rather than force adherence to a mandate in our constitution, I decided to tackle the problem by addressing the creed directly in the occasional summer preaching series, taking certain clauses of the creed and interpreting them in light of contemporary theologies, feminist and ecological among others. In the Baltimore church, for example, I used Elizabeth Johnson's *She Who Is: The Mystery of God in Feminist Theological Discourse* as a conversation partner for interpreting the creed, taking advantage of an opportunity to introduce congregation members to Johnson's very fine book.

My most successful engagement with the creed was in my Washington church, where we correlated preaching and education. We also recited the creed during worship (a new practice to many within the congregation). Over the course of three months, approximately fifty people (individually and in groups) read Justo González's *The Apostles' Creed for Today*. As they were reading, I did my best to preach on the creed's relevance for our life together and in mission to the community around us, highlighting points of correspondence between the life of the early church and our own. Engagement with the creed and with González's book over the course of several weeks stimulated vigorous reflection and conversation for a church in the nation's capital (as I'm sure it would for any church enmeshed in American political life), because González does a particularly good job of illumining the imperial context of early church life in the first two centuries of its existence and the church's understanding of this context as a political and socioeconomically debilitating environment.

Most scholars think the Apostles' Creed came into existence in Rome sometime in the second century to accompany the sacrament of baptism, during which the one to be baptized professed Jesus Christ as Lord and Savior.[14] So I invited people, residents of the nation's capital, to imagine what it would have been like to reside in the capital city of the Roman Empire, where anybody who was anybody served in the bureaucracy of the empire and where such service entailed pledging your allegiance to the only political party in town and professing Caesar as Lord. Then I invited them to imagine a small sect of folk who called themselves Christians and worshiped in a house church, perhaps just a couple of blocks from Caesar's palace. (The New York Avenue Presbyterian Church is two blocks from the White House.) As they baptized new members into the Christian faith, those baptized professed faith in a different Lord—Jesus the Messiah, who had been crucified as an enemy of the state. And why did they make such an outlandish profession of faith? Because they believed that he had been raised by God from death—that love beaten and crushed into the ground rises again to rule the world. Such a faith would surely have been regarded by others as deranged, but it was radical enough to sustain life amid all that threatened it.

There are of course reasons why some modern people might find the Apostles' Creed arcane and are inclined to relegate it to the dustbin of the Christian past. There are notions in the creed that many modern people dismiss as incomprehensible and outlandish: notions like the virgin birth, descent into hell, or ascension into heaven. But what I have tried to communicate in my preaching and teaching of the Apostles' Creed is that we recite the "I believe" not in order to pledge allegiance to doctrine but rather to affirm faith in Christ-shaped love—love that was crucified but has risen again and continues to be the ultimate reality of every moment of our Christian lives. And I have found that when explained in such a manner, people who might have been alienated by the Apostles' Creed find that they can embrace it as a powerful affirmation to make in the distrustful, polarized, apathetic, sometimes tyrannical, and often-bigoted world in which they live.

I have also found that there are affirmations in the creed that require extra attention, and chief among them is the notion of judgment. Time and again I've had to address someone's revulsion to the clause of the creed that affirms "from thence he shall come to judge the quick and the dead." What follows is a sermon that I preached on this particular clause. The context for this sermon is important. It was delivered on a Sunday during Stewardship Season on which the Stewardship Committee had invited representatives from each of the ministries of the church to set up displays that would feature their respective ministries and invite others to consider contributing their time and gifts.

TUNE UP

Philippians 2:5–11
Ephesians 4:1–10

If I had to identify the clause from the Apostles' Creed that has been the most difficult for me to wrap my head around, it would be this one: "from thence he shall come to judge the quick and the dead." In fact, it has been a stumbling block in my life of faith—one that has tormented me spiritually and psychologically! The root of my problem can be traced back to my early religious life. During my evangelical days as a Southern Baptist, revival preachers would come to my church to put the fear of God in us, specifying exactly what we needed to do to escape eternal damnation. These experiences left a scar on my soul. I now even have an expression for such teaching: "spiritual terrorism." To be sure, I learned plenty about the love of God in my days as an evangelical youth, and for that I am grateful. But when I embarked on a new spiritual journey as a Presbyterian, I began avoiding, running from notions like hell, eternal damnation, and judgment—so much so that about twenty years ago a fellow Presbyterian and clergy friend of mine said to me, "Roger, you are tolerant to a fault!" I thought long and hard about that comment and realized that somehow I had to make sense of Christian teaching on judgment, lest my brains fall out!

And this is what I've learned. As with every affirmation of the Apostles' Creed, context is critical to understanding—not just the context of the creed itself but also that of the biblical narrative out of which it emerged. It is vital to understand that the one who will come to judge the living and the dead is none other than Jesus—and what does the biblical narrative tell us about who he is? What the Bible tells us is that he attended to the sick, fed multitudes, announced good news to the poor and freedom for those captive or oppressed, and celebrated meals and friendship with sinners and tax collectors. He also told stories—one about a waiting father longing for a prodigal son to come home and another about a good Samaritan who used his resources to help a battered stranger in need. So for the poor, the broken, the imprisoned and tortured, the scorned and despised, for all those deprived of dignity, for all those who yearn for friendship or who hunger and thirst for the justice of God, the affirmation that it is **Jesus** who is coming to judge the living and the dead is good news—very good news, indeed!

And there is more. The creed affirms that this coming one, who was crucified by a Roman tyrant, "descended into hell" and then "ascended into heaven" and now reigns as Lord of all. And what does the biblical narrative tell us about the nature of his sovereignty? It conveys that he rules all of reality with love—a love based on justice that brings freedom through forgiveness, healing, restitution, and reconciliation where there is estrangement and enmity. This is the pattern of God in Christ that the author of Ephesians describes as "filling all things"—the entirety of the cosmos—all of which is poetic language for the ultimate reality with which we have to deal every moment of our lives. In short, the ultimate reality with which we have to deal is not a God of vengeance (as I once presumed) but the God who we know in Jesus Christ, whose trajectory in the world is one of justice, reconciliation, mercy, and love.

But there is something else that also needs to be said about his particular clause in the Apostles' Creed. Note that the creed refers to judgment as a future reality: "from thence he **will** come to judge the quick and the dead." This future orientation affirms that despite all evidence to the contrary, the future will be shaped like Jesus: it affirms that everything that fills the cosmos will be patterned after him. What this means is that there will be no future without justice for the poor, there will be no future that does not end in forgiveness, and there will be no future that does not end in reconciliation. In sum, love and justice are the only possible future for those who put their faith in the God made known to us in Jesus whose pattern of life fills the cosmos and shapes the future. It was this kind of faith that led Martin Luther King Jr. to affirm—even amidst beating, arrests, defamations of character, bombings and threats of assassination—that "the arc of the universe is long but it bends toward justice." In my mind, King's words are another way of affirming this clause in the creed—"from thence he shall come to judge the quick and the dead." In other words, this clause does not convey punishment or revenge but rather a radically different model of judgment. It promises a future in which things will be set right, when the *shalom*, the peace and harmony that God intends for the universe, will find fulfillment. Jesus rules as judge as God's bellwether, sounding a clear note of justice and love for the future.

As most of you know, I've been learning to play the guitar over the last eight years and have come to realize that while there are many skills that need to be acquired, none is more essential than learning to tune the instrument. Digital wonders have made this relatively easy. There is a smart phone application named Pro Tune that does a great job tuning your guitar. It only costs $1.99 and is worth every cent. But while this makes tuning one's guitar relatively easy, keeping it in tune is not. If it is too hot, the guitar goes out of tune; if it is too cold, it goes out of tune; if the temperature is moderate, it goes out of tune; if the humidity is too low, it goes out of tune; if the humidity is too high, it goes out of tune; if the humidity is just right, it goes out of tune; if your fingers are sweaty, it goes out of tune; if you use too much force when playing, it goes out of tune; if you look at it the wrong way, it goes out of tune; if you tune up your guitar in a perfectly climate-controlled room and then hold your breath and think only good thoughts, it stills goes out of tune! So I wasn't surprised when, during my first lesson with my new teacher, after playing just a few notes, he observed, "your guitar is out of tune." But then, to my amazement, he took my guitar and, without the benefit of any electric device, he hit a tuning fork on his knee and placed it to his ear and began a mystifying process of tuning the guitar using the harmonics on the fifth, seventh, and twelfth frets, listening to vibrations from the strings and then playing varied chords, in major and minor keys, and adjusting the tuning at each step along the way. He then handed it back to me, perfectly tuned. Well, I must have had a baffled look on my face, like, "Who is this guy? A magician or a dinosaur!?" So I proudly showed him my iPhone app, and he responded, "Very nice, but when you don't have your phone with you, you will always have your ear. And, more importantly, you must develop your 'ear' to know when your guitar is out of tune and what to do about it." Then he told me about a YouTube video that I should watch. It was a video of Andrés Segovia playing a piece from the Bach Lute Suites when mid-piece he sensed that his guitar had gone out of tune ever so slightly. So, literally without missing a beat, he reached up to one of the tuning pegs and gave it a slight twist and then kept playing, without a hint of hesitation. A master at work!

So how do you develop an ear like that of Segovia or the vision of the arc of the universe that Martin Luther King Jr. never lost sight of? **Practice and profess, profess and practice.** In Segovia's case, he developed his ear by committing hours to practice, guided by his conviction that beautiful music was possible. In King's case, visionary insight, his ability to perceive the arc of the universe and to anticipate a Christ-shaped future, was nurtured in his home and in the church. It emerged out of the historic faith of the universal church, confessed through the ages in the Apostles' Creed. And it emerged out of the corporate life, faith, and ministry of the black church in particular—from a community that professed and practiced Christian faith within a dangerous, racist, and hate-filled world.

That guiding vision of the arc of the universe that bends toward justice is nurtured within the corporate life and faith of The New York Avenue Presbyterian Church as well, every time we gather here for worship and every time we recite together the Apostles' Creed: "from thence he will come to judge the living and the dead." Think of the creed as a tuning fork that aligns our faith and hope with the historic faith and hope of the universal church, professed through the ages. We are further fine-tuned by all the ministries that we engage together. Today following worship, in the Peter Marshall Hall, you will find displays of the many ministries of our church. They range from education to worship, from Havana to Nairobi, from varied social ministries with at-risk people within our surrounding community to the library ministry under our roof. So after the worship service, you are invited to visit these displays where you can see and learn more about the many ministries of this congregation. Perhaps you will find one to which you wish to contribute your time, gifts, and talents, for it is in our shared life, faith, and ministry that we are fine-tuned—that we develop ears to hear and eyes to discern God's movement in our world and join in at those points where a Christ-shaped future is struggling toward realization now.

Amen.

In my preaching and teaching of the Apostles' Creed, and in many conversations with members of my congregations about it, I have learned more than I ever would have imagined that can enrich and revitalize the life and work of a socially engaged urban parish. "Teaching moments" have emerged throughout congregational engagement with the creed that we would not have encountered otherwise. As I have deployed the rich theological resources of the Christian tradition in my practice of ministry, including its creedal statements, I am constantly reminded of the Gospel of John's vivid presentation of the work of the Spirit or Paraclete in our midst—work that John describes as "both conserving and creative."[15] On the one hand, it is "conserving," for Jesus promises that the Spirit will "remind you of all that I have said to you" (John 14:26)—which is to say that it brings to our remembrance the story of God's incarnate Word in the world and keeps us grounded in the tradition of that Word. On the other hand, the Spirit's work is also "creative," for Jesus promises that it will "guide you into all truth . . . and declare to you the things that are to come" (16:13)—which is to say that the Spirit also reveals to us the mind of Christ in new situations, in every new time and place. The creative and conserving dimensions of the work of the Spirit among us are both vital, because too often we conserve without any sense for the new thing that God is doing or we create without any sense for the wisdom of the past. We need both the wisdom of the past—the rich theological resources of our tradition—as well as creative empowerment in the present to do God's reformed and reforming work; and according to John's Gospel, we can count on the promise that this is the Spirit's work in our midst.

Christian Triumphalism

Doing theology in the church and facilitating engagement with the rich theological resources of the Christian tradition is essential, because it helps people make sense of their own lives of discipleship and of the church's life and mission in the world. Traditional Christian affirmations, such as those articulated in the Apostles' Creed, have a vital role to play in the lives and ministries of urban Christians. But some traditional affirmations evoke teaching moments on another front because urban Christians are more likely than any Christians in America to encounter, on a daily basis, folk of other religious faiths. Thus, many have very serious concerns about Christian triumphalism. Questions invariably arise: What are they to make of the traditional teaching that Christ is the only way to salvation? Doesn't exclusivism threaten to stifle our work in the world, especially our work in partnership with non-Christians? These are burning questions for many urban Christians, and grappling with them is essential. They have usually encountered vehement articulations of the view that Christ is the only way to salvation; they have also encountered the "many paths to the same goal" approach to religious pluralism. In this section, I share something of the teaching moments that have evolved around their questions and concerns and my efforts to propose a path that takes a different course.

Christian triumphalism's center of gravity, past and present, is a single verse in the Gospel of John where Jesus declares, "I am the way, and the truth, and the life. No one comes to the Father except through me" (14:6). These have become fighting words among Christians, and in some circles they present a litmus test of orthodoxy; and probably no verse of Scripture has been used more often as a weapon with which to bludgeon non-Christians. Thus careful attention to this text must play a role in any engagement with questions of religious pluralism.

Biblical scholar Gail O'Day helpfully observes that John 14:1–6 is problematic when it is used to speak to questions that were never within the Gospel's purview:

> To use these verses in a battle over the relative merits of the world's religions is to distort their theological heart. . . . The Fourth Gospel is not concerned with the fate, for example, of Muslims, Hindus, or Buddhists, nor with the superiority or inferiority of Judaism and Christianity as they are configured in the modern world. These verses are the confessional celebration of a particular faith community, convinced of the truth and life it has received in the incarnation. The Fourth Evangelist's primary concern was the clarification and celebration of what it means to believe in Jesus (14:1, 10–11).[16]

Commentator David Rensberger also reminds us that the early Christian movement that produced the Gospel of John was not a world religion but a small, relatively powerless sect within a vast Roman Empire. They were, in other words, a group of believers in need of secure footing.[17] In this context, the affirmation of John 14:6 conveys pastoral words of comfort and assurance that they have access, through Jesus, to a sure and clear way to the life and love of God. In our day, these words can also provide assurance of access to divine reality—assurance that Jesus reveals the love of God and the meaning of human existence in relation to its gracious creator. Lord knows we need such assurance, and a path to follow—the one embodied by Jesus—as we make our way in the world among dangers. We need such assurance when it seems that all around us is falling apart. Like those early believers, we also need a particular place to stand in the world—a clear sense of our identity as followers of Jesus and of what it means to believe in him.

Still, there is no denying that John 14:6, particularly the latter half of it ("no one comes to the Father except by me"), can be, and has been, construed in exclusionary ways. But the cosmic perspective of John's Gospel provides intriguing food for thought. That cosmic perspective is expressed in the opening words of the Gospel: "In the beginning was the Word, and the Word was with God, and the Word was God. . . . And the Word became flesh and lived among us" (John 1:1, 14). Doug Ottati has called attention to insightful commentary on these verses in a very unlikely place: John Calvin's *Institutes of the Christian Religion*. Though Calvin is one of my patron saints, his theology is not a place I would have thought to turn for wisdom on the subject of religious pluralism! Yet in book 2 of the *Institutes*, Calvin, commenting on the prologue of John's Gospel, says that it is absurd to think "that if the Word of God became flesh, then he was confined within the narrow prison of an earthly body. . . . The Son of God descended from Heaven in such a way that, without leaving heaven, he willed to be borne in the virgin's womb, to go about the earth, and to hang upon the cross; yet he continuously filled the world even as he had done from the beginning."[18] In other words, as Ottati points out, Calvin affirms that God is truly present in Jesus but not exhausted in him.[19] Now that is an intriguing idea as one ponders the challenge of religious pluralism. Why? If God is genuinely present in the finite, yet not exhausted therein, then we can affirm the radical particularity of the Christian faith while remaining open to the possibility that the cosmic Word of God, which is genuinely present but not exhausted in Christ, may be at work in the faith of another. Biblical scholar Alan Culpepper makes a similar observation about John's presentation of the cosmic Christ:

> The exclusivist claims of the Fourth Gospel . . . must therefore be understood in the context of the opening claim that the revelation that came through Jesus Christ is the same as that which is universally present in the Logos. . . . Because the Gospel presents Jesus as the incarnation who made known the work of the Logos from the creation and through all time, it undercuts the triumphalism of claims that Christendom has a monopoly on the revelation of God. . . . John's Logos Christology allows Christians to affirm that adherents of other religious traditions may come to know God through the work of the Cosmic Christ.[20]

Now some will have questions about this: "It's a noble idea, but haven't you given up on the uniqueness of Christ? Haven't you given up on an orthodox tenet of faith—that God is known only in Christ and that salvation is found only in him?" No, because as a Christian I have come to know God through the particularity of Jesus Christ, the Word who became flesh in a specific time and place and who is confessed as Lord in a particular community of faith that seeks to embody his way in the world. I also believe that it is only within such a community that I can plumb the depths of my faith and come to know the inexhaustible cruciform love of God that can never be grasped completely by my limited understandings of it. I will be the first to admit that a local community of faith can be stingy, narrow, and even bigoted on occasion. But even when the church is at its worst, there are still moments wherein love overflows its bounds and a spirit of amazing grace speaks to the inexhaustible cruciform love of God. Paul spoke of the "treasure" of the gospel as something we embody in "earthen vessels" (2 Cor. 4:7), and admittedly the vessel is regrettably all too earthy! Yet my faith in the "treasure" embodied in the church gives me confidence that it is a place where I will continue to experience an inexhaustible love that overflows the bounds of the institution and my grasp. Thus, when I encounter a person of another faith, I can experience that person as an object of God's love and also as a person in whose faith the cosmic Christ, who is not exhausted by my limited grasp of it, is at work in a way that opens revelatory possibilities for me.

This is not the same thing as the "many paths to the same goal" approach to religious pluralism. So how do I respond when someone comes to me with some variation of the following questions: "Don't you think that there are many paths to the same goal? Shouldn't we explore as many different paths as we can since they are headed to the same ultimate destination?" I attempt to say something like this: "I agree that we ought to respect other religious traditions and try to understand as much as we can about the faith of others, but I find following Jesus a more than sufficient challenge, one that requires everything I have. I also think that humility is called for whenever we speak of the mystery of God, and that it would be presumptuous to assume that I know the ultimate goal of all religious traditions. However, as I endeavor to follow Jesus, my experience of the inexhaustible cruciform love of God leads me to believe that divine reality can never be confined to the narrow prism of my particular faith, and thus I must be open to the possibility of encountering God at work in the faith of another."

In my work with people of other religious faiths within interfaith organizations, as well as IAF affiliations like WIN, I often sense the inexhaustible love of God at work in our partnership and all of the redemptive possibilities therein. Moreover, theologian Ted Jennings provides intriguing food for thought when he observes that secular nonviolent movements such as the one in Tiananmen Square in 1989 or movements to abolish torture show forth the power of the cross to transform history.[21] These movements can be places where Christians discern the cruciform God at work in the world. Indeed, crosses litter the landscape and are for me cruciform places where we can work with people of other religious faiths or people without religious affiliation. Political theorist Michael Walzer provides a wonderful image for such work: we "can acknowledge each other's different ways, respond to each other's cries for help, learn from each other, and march (sometimes) in each other's parades."[22] I believe this is a foundation from which Christians can move into the public square and partner with others in the holy work of mending the creation.

Questions for Further Reflection

Do you agree or disagree with Doug Ottati's perception that too often theology is ancillary to what we perceive as more important tasks of ministry?

Where do you stand on the issue of using cultural wisdom such as community organizing, the best practices of business management, or therapeutic wisdom for the life of the church? How do you understand the relationship between Christ and culture? What do you think of this criterion for the use of cultural wisdom: worldly wisdom is most useful when it aids us in discerning the places where God is bringing life out of brokenness?

Do you think of "self-interest" as a positive or problematic concept? What new insights did you gain from the discussion of self-interest, or what questions did it raise for you?

What does reciting the Apostles' Creed mean to you? Which affirmations are most significant to you? Which raise the most questions for you? What role does the Apostles' Creed (and other creeds that may be part of your confessional tradition) play in your own life of discipleship and that of your congregation? How might you deepen your engagement with them?

In what contexts have you encountered John 14:6 ("I am the resurrection and the life; no one comes to the Father except through me")? What have you learned from these encounters? How would you articulate your understanding of this text and its implications? What questions does it raise for you? How has interaction with people of other religious faiths impacted your experience and that of your congregation?

Of the four issues engaged in this chapter—Christ and culture, self-interest, creeds, or religious pluralism—which is most important to you and why? Which do you find the most challenging in your own life of faith and that of your congregation?

Chapter 6

Talking about Race and Poverty in the City

In the mid 1990s, during the time that I was serving on the clergy leadership team of BUILD (Baltimoreans United in Leadership Development, a church-based community organizing affiliate of IAF), Rev. Curtis Jones, a fellow Presbyterian pastor and leader in the National Presbyterian Black Caucus, gathered a small group of BUILD pastors to talk about racism. We read and discussed several articles on racism and agreed that it would be good to broaden the conversation. But the conversation never found traction within the larger organization, and the reason was philosophical. Instead of talking about race, BUILD defined its purpose as doing something about it and had successfully addressed more issues facing the majority African American population in Baltimore than any other organization in the city. We had successfully addressed education reform, after-school programming, and affordable housing. We had pushed the city council and the mayor to pass the first city service contract living-wage bill in the country. And whites and blacks stood shoulder-to-shoulder in all of these endeavors. We learned each other's stories and came to respect one another. Yet, except for that initial foray into the topic by a small group of pastors, we never managed to get a sustained conversation about race off the ground.

The issue of race and poverty in urban America continued to haunt me years later when I moved forty miles down the road to Washington, D.C., and came to realize that it was even more racially divided than Baltimore. It is an open wound in the nation's capital—and the country as a whole—that some acknowledge but few address. Most Americans would acknowledge racism as a blight on our historical past, but many would argue that we've come a long way since the days of slavery, Jim Crow, and the civil rights movement. After all, a black man has now been elected *twice* as president of the United States. Others, however, are not as sanguine and regard racism as a central plight of our present and not just a relic of the past, and I find myself among them. Racism suffuses current political debates on immigration, health care, jobs, wealth, and poverty. And in our major urban areas, race is an undercurrent of daily existence. Within the Washington Interfaith Network (WIN, Washington's IAF affiliate organization), conversations bubbled up again and again about addressing the issue of racism. To get the ball rolling, three of us, pastors of three District churches, began to explore the possibility of partnering for such an endeavor. Lionel Edmonds, Pastor of the Mt. Lebanon Baptist Church, Joe Daniels, Pastor of the Emory United Methodist Church, and I were hopeful that our three congregations—two largely black and one largely white—might be willing to come together for sustained discussion and reflection on the reality of racism and its impact on our city and our lives. We broached the possibility with our congregations, who enthusiastically concurred and committed to undertaking such an initiative.

Within my own congregation, our McClendon Scholar-in-Residence Board had wholeheartedly endorsed and supported the idea. This group was formed to address issues of theological substance within the church and community around us, and they discerned that none was more pressing than racism and poverty. Thus we began meeting with Joe and Lionel (and members of their congregations) in order to chart the course ahead. To kick off the conversations, our three congregations sponsored a series of lectures by Dr. Brian Blount on the book of Revelation from an African American perspective. Blount, a distinguished African American New Testament scholar and President of Union Presbyterian Seminary (Richmond, Virginia), had authored several books on cultural hermeneutics and the book of Revelation in particular, and his lectures were stimulating and powerful, sparking a conversation on race around the most enigmatic book of the Bible. We then planned to plunge into sustained study together of theologian James Cone's stunning book *The Cross and the Lynching Tree*, which examines the two most emotionally charged symbols in the history of the African American community. Cone, a distinguished professor of systematic theology at Union Theological Seminary in New York, is the dean of the black theology movement in America and a perceptive interpreter of faith, race, and the American experience. We anticipated that his book would provide rich food for thought and conversation among members of our congregations as we explored our experience of racism and poverty in Washington, D.C.

We decided to plan a Lenten series based on Cone's book and to forge a covenant among our three congregations to read the book and engage a conversation on race and poverty in Washington D.C. We planned to launch our joint Lenten venture on the Sunday before Martin Luther King's birthday with an afternoon worship service honoring our covenant that would feature choral music from the choirs of each of the three congregations. Three dates during Lent were scheduled for the sessions during which members of our three congregations would meet to reflect together on their reading of Cone's book. We also contacted Dr. Cone, who was intrigued by our joint venture and graciously agreed to travel to Washington to meet with us in May of that year, after we had completed our reading and discussion of his whole book. Soon thereafter we began to advertise the service and the Lenten discussions. The books were ordered and brochures were printed. *The Washington Post* took notice of our plans and featured an article about our upcoming Lenten venture, which had the effect of drawing people from other neighboring churches within the D.C. community who wanted to participate.

On Epiphany Sunday 2013, as the launch of our joint study venture drew near, I decided to engage the topic of racism and address our upcoming Lenten plans in my preaching. The Magi of Matthew's Gospel seemed to me to be a rich biblical resource for reflection as we approached a conversation on race. Here is the sermon.

TODAY'S MAGI

Matthew 2:1–12
Isaiah 60:1–6

Throughout the centuries the magi have been subject to remarkable legendary development. The Gospel of Matthew simply reports that "wise men from the East came to Jerusalem"—or at least that is the NRSV translation of the original Greek text. The Greek text simply uses the word "magi," a word that doesn't actually specify whether they were men or women. All Matthew tells us is that "magi from the East came to Jerusalem." But think how much more we know about this crew as a result of popular imagination! We know their names, their number (three), their ethnicity, and their mode of transportation—although in Matthew there is not a camel anywhere in sight. They've been elevated from astrologers to royalty—kings, no less; their gifts of gold, frankincense, and myrrh have become symbolic of all kinds of Christian virtues; and their relics have scattered well beyond the Middle East. In fact, Raymond Brown, the preeminent scholar of the Gospel infancy narratives, contends that their relics have traveled more widely than the wise men themselves ever thought about traveling.[1]

But the truth of the matter is that despite the popularity of the Christmas carol, "We Three Kings," they probably weren't kings at all, but were more likely servants of kings. In fact, New Testament scholar Mark Alan Powell, after reviewing all the evidence in Greco-Roman and Jewish literature, points out that the only connection to kings in Matthew's story is one of *contrast*, because magi were invariably depicted as folk who lacked personal or political power and were more likely servants of kings. They performed functions for the benefits of the monarchs they served, frequently tyrants who exercised capricious and total control over their fortunes. Thus, they also are often depicted as victims of abuse on account of their servile status. This, Powell suggests, is how Matthew's first-century congregation would have thought of them, given this standard depiction of them—as servants of kings who were altogether likely to have known from personal experience the degradations of serving an oppressor.[2] So what were the magi looking for? What did they anticipate finding as they followed that star? Their question is this: "Where is the child who was born king of the Jews? We want to pay him homage." Why? Were they hoping for a different kind of political order, a different kind of kingdom—one that did not endorse servitude or other forms of abuse? Were they longing for a different kind of politics? Was this why they wanted to find and venerate this child?

And there are still other things to ponder about their presence. There is no question that these servant magi represent the racial and ethnic Other in Matthew's account of Jesus' birth. They were outsiders—what some would call pagan or heathen. Scholars continue to debate where they hailed from, but most contend they were from either Persia (that is, present-day Iran), or Babylonia (present-day Iraq). Though some prefer to describe them as Arabs—from the Arabian desert regions. So—Iranians, Iraqis, or Arabs—you can take your pick as you picture in your mind's eye the outsiders who kneel so reverently before the newborn king of the Jews. Whichever the case may be, they represent the fulfillment of a biblical promise made to Abraham and Sarah that from their seed would come a people who would be a blessing to all the families of the earth. It is a promise reiterated in our morning Scripture lesson from the prophet Isaiah, who predicts that in the homecoming of the exiled people of Israel, all the nations of the earth will find homecoming. And the word for "nations" in Isaiah is an important one: it is *goyim,* or Gentiles: that is, non-Jews. So here at the beginning of his Gospel, Matthew takes up this same radically inclusive vision in this snapshot of the racially Other magi worshiping the Jewish Jesus. And then, as if to add a final exclamation mark to this point,

Jesus, in the closing scene of Matthew's Gospel, commissions his disciples, "Go, and make disciples of all nations"—of all the *goyim*—all the non-Jews (28:19). Soon thereafter, Paul took up this commission as the very heart of his vocation as apostle to the Gentiles, as one called to extend the promise made to Israel to all the nations. On this Epiphany Sunday, Matthew's magi—these racially ethnic "outsiders"—arrive to remind us of the fulfillment of that promise in the coming of Christ. They represent the radical inclusion of all races in the ultimate blessing God has in mind for the whole world.

But if this is what the magi represent in Matthew, here is a sad truth of Christian history: this biblical vision of radical divine hospitality and inclusion quickly became racist and exclusionary. Exclusion began in the second or third centuries with the teaching of supersessionism. The new covenant established in Jesus was said to supersede—that is, to replace—God's old covenant with Israel. To put it bluntly, Christianity replaced Judaism in the purposes of God. In the Christian West, the teaching of supersessionism prevailed for two thousand years, with virulent effects, as European Christians organized pogroms against the Jews. And in the years leading up to the Holocaust, German churches denied that Jesus was even Jewish! What a tragic reversal of Matthew's inclusive vision. The Jews became the outsiders, and the Gentiles became the insiders and oppressors of Jews. In other words, Western European Christianity took on a racist character, and Matthew's vision of inclusion was perverted. But the Jews, of course, were not the only targets of racism. The descendants of Noah's son Ham, whom Noah cursed, came to be identified with Africans, who thus also became targets of European and American Christian racism.[3] What a tragic reversal of Matthew's vision! Yet, sadly, the historical facts speak for themselves.[4]

So what should we do? If the scourge of racism is a tragic part of our history, then the question is, How do we address it? As I've pondered this question, I'm captivated by what the *Christian Century* magazine dubs "the New Black Theology" that is emerging, spearheaded by black theologians like Kameron Carter and Willie Jennings of Duke Divinity School. Carter and Jennings make the startling claim that modern racism corresponds to early Christian debates about heretical movements like Gnosticism. For you see, the gnostics propagated a version of Christ and Christianity that amputated its Jewish roots. The gnostics severed Jesus from Judaism. In response to this theological danger, a second-century theologian named Irenaeus argued the opposite case convincingly, contending that Jesus' covenantal Jewish flesh counts.[5] Kameron Carter and Willie Jennings, who agree with Irenaeus on this point, draw on these early debates to insist that a fully embodied Jesus matters, because **"Jewish flesh is most authentically itself when it welcomes the Gentile."**[6] Hospitality, they argue, is the core of Jewish identity. So the church, in their view, is called to do the same. Indeed, Carter and Jennings argue that Christianity's failure—its racism—is a forfeiture of its Jewishness, and a failure of Western Christianity in particular, as it long debated whether non-Europeans and Jews were even included in God's covenant. But they contend that the racist history of Western Christianity can be reversed by a deep affirmation of God in Christ who became Jewish flesh to extend the covenant of Israel to the nations.[7] It is a fascinating argument, isn't it? That by embracing Jesus' Jewishness, like the magi of Matthew's story, we grasp a radically inclusive vision of a God whose purposes embrace racial Others.

So I find myself wondering on this Epiphany Sunday: If Matthew's magi, who kneel so reverently before the newborn king of the Jews, represent the divine vision of racial inclusion and confrontation with the politics of oppression, then what is their significance for us—for American Christians bound by a history of racism? Can they help twenty-first-century European American Christians embrace our Jewish roots and our God-given vocation as a people of radical hospitality? For it seems to me that the magi are not real until we can claim them as part of our history, as our forebears in the faith; for the fact of the matter is that all of us here today are *goyim*, Gentiles, strangers to the covenants of promise, wild branches who by the grace of God in Christ have been grafted onto Israel's cultivated olive tree! The magi in Matthew, racial outsiders and probably servants of tyrannical royal masters, travel from afar to worship Jesus and compel us on this Epiphany Sunday to reflect on the radical hospitality of God in Christ. They also compel us to ask the question, Who are the magi in our own midst? A number of possibilities suggest themselves, but perhaps none more so than those who were forced to travel across the Atlantic from far countries in chains to toil in the New World as slaves of cruel masters. Perhaps they and their descendants are among our American magi, whose history painfully exposes the racism at the core of our national and religious life. Many speak of slavery as America's greatest sin—even its original sin. And as residents of this city—the nation's capital—know all too well, its painful legacy is with us still. Which is why, on the near horizon, during the upcoming season of Lent, this congregation will be making its way to the cross in the company of two neighboring African American congregations, reading and reflecting together on theologian James Cone's powerful book, titled *The Cross and the Lynching Tree*—the two most emotionally charged symbols in the history of the African American community.

In this book, James Cone brings to our remembrance the lynching, torture, and burnings of thousands of black people and of a country that ignored these atrocities. And he invites us to rethink the theology of the cross and its redemptive power for us. Cone contends that Christianity took hold in black hearts, not because of the white man's missionary efforts, but because they found in the cross of Jesus the reflection of their own suffering and hope in a God of resurrection. Moreover, Cone argues that the cross and the lynching tree bind white and black in an American tragedy and in hope beyond tragedy. In fact, he says this:

> What happened to blacks also happened to whites. When whites lynched blacks, they were literally lynching themselves—their sons, daughters, cousins . . . . We are bound together in America by faith and tragedy. . . . All the hatred we have expressed toward one another cannot destroy the profound mutual love and solidarity that flow deeply between us—a love that empowered blacks to open their arms to receive the many whites who were empowered by the same love to risk their lives in the black struggle for freedom. No two people in America have had more violent and loving encounters than black and white people. . . . No gulf between blacks and whites is too great to overcome. . . . If America has the courage to confront the great sin and ongoing legacy of white supremacy with repentance and reparation there is hope "beyond tragedy."[8]

I think of Matthew's magi as forerunners of all who have perceived in Jesus a different kind of politics—one that heals through justice and reconciliation; one with the power to create the Beloved Community that Martin Luther King Jr. so yearned for. King's dream still beckons us if we can only face into the crosses that still litter the landscape of our history and our lives and trust in God's power to bring life out of death. An extraordinary journey through Lent awaits us. And on this Sunday of Epiphany, as we anticipate it, we are invited to celebrate with the magi the birth of Jesus Christ. Come kneel with them in worship before him and offer the best gifts you have in faithful service to him—for his birth, his life, his death and resurrection summon us to participate, by divine grace at work within us, in God's radical hospitality—in the cosmic, reconciling purposes of God. Amen.

On the very next Sunday, the afternoon of January 20, 2013—the day before the celebration of Martin Luther King's birthday and the Second Inauguration of Barack Obama as President of the United States—our three congregations joined together for a celebratory concert and covenanting service that initiated our conversations on race and poverty in Washington, D.C. By common agreement, the service was held at the predominantly white church, The New York Avenue Presbyterian Church. My two black colleagues felt strongly that the service should be held at New York Avenue. On several occasions leading up to this day, Joe and Lionel had firmly stated that white folk needed to take the lead in this matter, because, as Joe put it, "when a white congregation addresses the issue of race people sit up and take notice!"

Holding this concert at New York Avenue church was a gutsy decision to make for another reason: it is located just two blocks from the White House, and parking was severely restricted in the twenty-four-hour period before the inauguration festivities were to begin the next day. Security for the inauguration was so tight that only a single parking garage was available to us to accommodate those who drove into the area; the rest would have to use the public metro services or walk. Notwithstanding, a robust six hundred worshipers showed up for the covenanting service and concert that featured lively choral music from the three churches. And more than 150 people covenanted to engage a sustained conversation on race during the season of Lent.

Why did we embark on this project? All three churches have been engaged in varied ministries in the community for years, working alongside others— black and white—to address homelessness, poverty, and jobs and to mentor at-risk youth, among other things. So why did we decide that we now also needed to talk about race? Were we proposing a conversation about race in order to address open wounds that have never been fully healed, never fully exposed, and that are perpetually with us? Were we proposing to talk about race in order to acknowledge and address America's original sin? These were among our motives, to be sure. But let me be more specific. My own deepest hope was that our conversation together might expose the very different ways in which we tell the American story and our faith stories—differences that might prove to be disruptive and destabilizing for us. Disruptive and destabilizing spaces are cross-shaped spaces from which new life can emerge.

One especially important concern was our understanding of the alluring, foundational American narrative that America was the new Israel, the promised land blessed by God—a nation of chosen people with a special destiny. This sense of being "chosen" was surely derived from the Puritans. Eighteenth-century theologian Jonathan Edwards, for example, clearly articulated this sense in a sermon in which he contended that the discovery of America, the American Revolution, and the religious revivals of the Great Awakening were signs that God had begun the creation of a new heaven and new earth in the new nation. In Lincoln's era, churches continued to articulate this understanding of national identity by teaching that America was God's "new Israel."[9] However, this paradigmatic notion of manifest destiny (as it came to be known) also legitimated slavery, the expulsion of native peoples from their land, and many of our wars. Abraham Lincoln was one of the few American presidents to resist this ideology when he described Americans as "the almost chosen people."[10] Then, in his second inaugural address he explicitly challenged the facile notion that God's ways could be identified with our ways, naming slavery as a scourge. Yet despite Lincoln's effort to correct any such presumption, the notion of special destiny (American exceptionalism) persists to this day. Which raises the question, How might American slaves have told the nation's founding story, and the Christian story, differently? Could we even hear the counter-narrative they might propose—one that might disrupt our sense of identity?

It is often assumed that slave religion represented acquiescent adoption of the master's religion, and thus slave Christianity served as an opiate for their plight. But in his groundbreaking study of slave religion, Joseph Raboteau completely debunks any such notion. Raboteau argues that American slaves and their descendants wove a different story out of the biblical story they received. According to Raboteau, they dismantled the myth of America as the new Israel—a new Israel with a special destiny—and they found in the biblical story of Israel in bondage in Egypt a reflection of their own story. Thus, for the slave, America was not the new Israel, but rather Egypt, the land of Pharaoh. In fact, one of the hymns in our hymnal, "Go Down, Moses," came from slave religion. "Go down Moses" (they sang) "and tell old Pharaoh to let my people go." When white folk sing this hymn, they may be unaware that the place of their ancestors in this hymn is in Pharaoh's court! Indeed, Raboteau says this: "it is an abiding and tragic irony of our national history that white America's claim to be a New Israel has been constantly denied by Old Israel still enslaved in her midst."[11]

Reflection on our understanding of America's founding narrative was essential, because any conversation about race in American requires acknowledgment of it. Any notion that we are the new Israel or someway *privileged* by God needs to be countered, disrupted, destabilized by the African American counter-narrative of slavery in Egypt, for both of these stories are tragically intertwined in our common life. But if we deeply understand and assimilate these contrasting, destabilizing narratives, then they will open up cross-shaped places from which justice, healing, redemption, and liberation will emerge.

I also hoped to prompt reflection on our understandings of the cross—on what it represents in our lives and culture—because this, too, was integral to any conversation we might have about race. When I was growing up in the Southern Baptist Church in the Midwest, the cross for me was a symbol of a private transaction between me and God by means of which my salvation and eternal life were secured. The story of the cross that I learned as a child conveyed that I was a sinner under the judgment of God, deserving of death; yet Jesus' sacrificial death on the cross placated and erased God's anger against me, and by this amazing grace I was saved and granted eternal life.

As my faith matured, I encountered more biblical understandings of the cross and came to embrace a much more public, rather than private, construal of it. The cross exposes the fact that the violent, death-tending ways of the world are *not* God's way in the world. Indeed, God's love and justice are at work in the world to bring life out of these death-tending perversions. Thus I embraced the cross not as a private affair or the means by which a wrathful deity was placated but rather as a public exposure of sin, revealing a God who reconciles enmity.

I have no doubt that my grasp of the cross would have expanded much earlier in my life if I had been in conversation with African American sisters and brothers in Christ about their own understanding of it—if I had been more aware of the crosses that litter the landscape of their world—crosses that were literally burning in their ancestors' front yards or hanging as "strange fruit" on a lynching tree. If I had been in such conversation, I also suspect I would have grasped much earlier Jesus' admonition to take up your cross daily and follow me (Luke 9:23)—words I am only beginning to understand. All three Synoptic Gospels contain this injunction, but only Luke adds the word "daily"— ". . . take up their crosses *daily* and follow me." In *The Cross and the Lynching Tree*, James Cone observes that Martin Luther King Jr. knew exactly what it meant to pick up his cross daily. From the time he accepted leadership in the movement to his last sermon in Memphis, King was "hounded by death": he knew he might be killed. He knew that every time he or his colleagues committed themselves to an action, they were literally committing their lives. King once said, "when I took up the cross I recognized its meaning. The cross is something you bear and ultimately that you die on." King knew well that picking up one's cross daily was a disruptive, destabilizing practice, yet one that opened up space in which one might grow strong and journey toward liberation: a person "dies when he [or she] refuses to stand up for what is right."[12] In short, we're going to die one way or another, so why not choose to pick up the cross daily and die so that we might live!

In sum, as we approached our Lenten conversations on race with covenant partners, I endeavored to prompt reflection on two foundational matters. One was the real tension between the prevailing understanding of the American founding narrative as the story of the new Israel with a manifest destiny and the contrasting, disruptive, destabilizing narrative of America as a story of slavery in Egypt. The second was the story of the cross in our lives and culture and what it might mean to pick up our crosses today, especially in our engagement with issues of race and poverty.

The Conversations

On Saturday morning February 9, 2013, 120 faithful members of Emory United Methodist, Mt. Lebanon Baptist, and New York Avenue Presbyterian gathered in the fellowship hall of the Emory church for our first discussion of race and poverty. (We were delighted that members of another downtown church, Luther Place, also wanted to take part in the conversation.) We came with great anticipation and no little anxiety to discuss the first chapter of James Cone's book — a chapter that spares no detail in its description of the horrific practice of lynching during the Jim Crow era of American history. Rev. Joe Daniels took responsibility for launching the two-hour session. He wisely decided to refrain from lecturing and quickly broke us up into small groups to discuss several questions. Chief among them was this one: "Do you see the cross and the lynching tree together? Why or why not?" Here is a quotation from Cone's first chapter that provides context for this question (a quote that all of the participants would have read):

> The more black people struggled against white supremacy, the more they found in the cross the spiritual power to resist the violence they so often suffered. . . . Just as Jesus did not deserve to suffer, they knew they did not deserve it; yet faith was the one thing white people could not control or take away. . . . They shouted, danced, clapped their hands and stomped their feet as they bore witness to the power of Jesus' cross which had given them an identity far more meaningful than the harm white supremacy could do them. No matter whose songs they sang or what church they belonged to, they infused them with their own experience of suffering and transformed what they received into their own. "Jesus Keep Me Near the Cross," "Must Jesus Bear the Cross Alone?" and other white Protestant evangelical hymns did not sound or feel the same when black and whites sang them because their life experiences were so different.[13]

Joe Daniels put us all at ease by assuring us that we were in a "safe space" for discussion and then sent us into our small group conversations. After an hour of discussion, we reconvened and Joe invited representatives from each group to share key questions and insights that emerged during the course of their conversation. Afterward we committed to do relational meetings with members of our small groups, prayed together, and closed the meeting. What follows is a sampling from the feedback recorded on evaluation forms assessing the first gathering:

When I came today, I thought . . .
    . . . I'm not sure of what to expect. Be open to whatever happens.
    . . . it was important to have conversations about race and faith, but I wasn't sure what to expect.
    . . . interracial conversations about faith are both painful and uncomfortable but necessary.
    . . . tempers were going to flare up and people wouldn't want to share in groups.
    . . . I wasn't sure how open and productive the discussions would be.
    . . . that it might have been difficult to say some of the things that I felt needed to be addressed.
    . . . I wasn't sure what to expect. I felt a certain amount of trepidation about where the conversation might lead.
Now I see . . .
    . . . others are willing to have open dialogue in a safe space.
    . . . how important it is to maintain hope and grow it together through sharing and developing action ideas.
    . . . the lynching tree extends beyond its original purpose.
    . . . that our differences can unite us, and we can become comfortable in discussing race without putting each other down.
    . . . that there are still lynching trees in other forms today.
    . . . that others of different cultural experiences were interested in hearing what I had to say or at least willing to consider my perspective.
    . . . I am very glad I came. It's been a gift to be here and engage in conversations with folks I would not otherwise have the opportunity to speak with.
    . . . I have a better understanding of how the cross and the lynching tree can bring about direct conversations on how we can make society better for all people.
Next time, I wish . . .
    . . . no change. I like the format. It allows for flowing conversations.
    . . . we would have more time to listen and absorb the views of other groups.
    . . . we could have time to tell our own stories of "race."
    . . . we met individually with more people we don't know.
    . . . we have more time for integrating our faith in our conversation.
    . . . to determine a concrete solution to approach this cultural divide that is the crux of our racial issues.

The second conversation took place at The New York Avenue Church on the evening of February 26. It was a rainy and cold night. Nevertheless, people had made a commitment to these conversations and showed up. In our first conversation, several folk had expressed interest in having an opening presentation to launch discussion, and as it was my time to lead I obliged them with a short one to provide a biblical framework for our reflection. The participants had been asked to read chapter 2 of Cone's book—a reflection on the work of the great theologian and social critic Reinhold Niebuhr and the deafening silence about the atrocity of lynching in his voluminous writing and public speaking. I confess that I was nervous during the presentation, not so much because the subject matter exposed a weakness in one of the great social prophets of the twentieth century but because I was addressing the issue of racism before a racially mixed audience. Nonetheless, I pressed ahead, unsure of my footing. I gave them a handout with the following quotations for reflection:

From *The Cross and the Lynching Tree*

Niebuhr had the "eyes to see" black suffering, but I believe he lacked the "heart to hear" it as his own. Although he wrote many essays about race, commenting on a variety of racial issues in America and Asia, the problem of race was never one of his central theological or political concerns. . . . It has always been difficult for white people to empathize fully with the experience of black people. But it has never been impossible.[14]

In 2001, the *Union Seminary Quarterly Review* featured an essay by Cone titled "Theology's Great Sin: Silence in the Face of White Supremacy," in which he articulated four reasons "why white theologians ignore racism":

(1) Most importantly, whites do not talk about racism because they do not have to talk about it; (2) White theologians avoid racial dialogue because talk about white supremacy arouses deep feelings of guilt; (3) because they do not want to engage black rage; and (4) Whites do not say much about racial justice because they are not prepared for a radical redistribution of wealth and power.[15]

I titled my introductory presentation, "The Recovery of Sight to the Blind," and read from Luke 4:16–20:

When he came to Nazareth, where he had been brought up, he went to the synagogue on the sabbath day, as was his custom. He stood up to read, and the scroll of the prophet Isaiah was given to him. He unrolled the scroll and found the place where it was written: "The Spirit of the Lord is upon me, because he has anointed me to bring good news to the poor. He has sent me to proclaim release to the captives and recovery of sight to the blind, to let the oppressed go free, to proclaim the year of the Lord's favor." And he rolled up the scroll, gave it back to the attendant, and sat down. The eyes of all in the synagogue were fixed on him.

I then proceeded to talk about racism in a colorblind society. I expressed my conviction that Niebuhr was not alone in his inability to see certain kinds of racism, for there are racist practices all around us that we often fail to see. For example, in her stunning book *The New Jim Crow*, Michelle Alexander chronicles an almost invisible atrocity—the deliberate reinstatement of Jim Crow under the racially neutral language of law and order, tough on crime and the war on drugs—a reality that has incarcerated hundreds of thousands if not millions of black men. Our national "War on Drugs" is largely responsible for this. In the last thirty years the U.S. penal population has exploded, swelling from three hundred thousand to more than two million, and drug convictions have been the primary reason. According to Alexander, this astonishing growth in the penal population represents an institutional effort to reinstate Jim Crow after its official demise on account of civil rights legislation. Consider the following: Studies demonstrate that people of all races use and sell illegal drugs, and they also suggest that white youth are more likely to engage in drug crimes than people of other colors. However, in many states, black men are admitted to prison for drug related crimes at rates twenty to fifty times greater than whites. Of the two million men in prison today, more than half are black, and in our major cities 80 percent of black men now have criminal records and are thus subject to legalized discrimination for the rest of their lives in terms of employment, housing discrimination, and denial of other rights, including the right to vote. In short, according to Michelle Alexander, Jim Crow is alive and well in an age when race is not supposed to make a difference.[16] Any remedy to this problem, she says, cannot avoid the issue of race—indeed, of structural and institutional racism. Segregated and unequal schools, segregated and jobless ghettos, and segregated public discourse will all need to be addressed. The remedy requires us to move beyond any presumption that our society is colorblind, because neutrality-based ideologies only serve to mask the problem.[17]

I then suggested that Luke's Gospel prompts us to move beyond colorblindness. Jesus inaugurates his ministry by appearing in his hometown synagogue and reading from the prophet Isaiah—words about good news for the poor, release of the captives, and recovery of sight for the blind. These words are a programmatic description of the ministry that is about to unfold. They convey Luke's understanding of the ministry and mission of Jesus in a nutshell, capturing the large canvas upon which Luke paints the Gospel story. On my first reading of this inaugural story, Jesus' announcement of "release of the captives" most captured my attention in light of Michelle Alexander's reflections on the new Jim Crow. But on a second reading, it was Jesus' announcement of "the recovery of sight for the blind" that grabbed me. According to commentators, Jesus is claiming as a mandate for his own ministry the ultimate prophetic vision—God's work of bringing light to the nations.[18]

I then called attention to a distinctive feature of the Gospel of Luke: Luke is the only Gospel with a sequel—the book of the Acts of the Apostles. And Acts begins with the story of Pentecost—of the multiracial, multilingual bringing of the gospel to the nations of the world. Pentecost is often interpreted as the reversal of ancient story of Babel of Genesis 11. So I briefly recalled this Genesis story, the great mythic account in which all humankind is represented as a single clan or tribe wandering aimlessly over the earth. Lest they be scattered over the face of the earth, they decide to build a tower that reaches into the heavens; and the stated reason for this building project is that they might "make a name" for themselves. Thus, the traditional interpretation is that the story is about human pride, and according to this interpretation, God's response to human arrogance is to scatter the people, to divide them, resulting in a multicultural and multilingual world. The problem with this interpretation, however, is that it comes very close to suggesting that human diversity and difference is a punishment from God. But biblical scholar Ted Hiebert has offered an alternative and more compelling interpretation. He points out that nowhere in the story is pride identified as the human problem and nowhere is God's response to the building project described as punishment. According to Hiebert, God's problem with this building project is not pride but rather cultural homogeneity. All the inhabitants of the earth speak one language and wish to live in one place, and God recognizes that the human race is intent on preserving one uniform culture. Thus God intervenes to introduce cultural difference, introducing multiple languages and dispersing people throughout the earth. In other words, diversity is God's intention for the world.[19]

Based on this interpretation, it would be incumbent on humankind to practice hospitality to the stranger. But here's the catch: human difference can also prompt alternative responses—the specters of hatred, division, and exploitation. And political, cultural, racial, and economic exploitation is clearly not what God intends because exploitation is really just another attempt to force difference into one homogenous mold. God intended for us to appreciate diversity and difference by welcoming the stranger.

This is why Luke's story of Pentecost is very good news. The early Christians realized that they would never learn to honor God's intentions for human difference without the empowering presence of God's Spirit. And so Luke's sequel—Acts —begins with a vivid tale about the gift of the Holy Spirit to the earliest Christians. The Spirit comes upon them in a sound of a "violent wind" from heaven as tongues of fire dance on the heads of the disciples and they utter United-Nations-styled proclamations, which are greeted with cries of amazement. The voice that is given to the church is, intriguingly, a decidedly multiethnic and multilingual one. In essence, the arrival of the Spirit does not abolish local cultures and customs in favor of some vague, one-size-fits-all message that floats above the real lives of people. In short, the Spirit's work in the world entails diversity and color. The question is, Can we see it?

This brought me back to the inaugural scene of Jesus' ministry and his reading from Isaiah about the recovery of sight to the blind. You've no doubt heard the old adage, "what you see is what you get." The trouble is, we don't see very well. We are, on the one hand, nearsighted—we often see only our kind or homogeneity. Our myopia can be racial, class-bound, even gender-bound. We find it difficult to see beyond our kin, so we often don't know the stories of folk who are racially different. On the other hand, we can also be farsighted, in that sometimes we can't see that which is close up, right under our noses: for example, the black men in our own city who are severely disenfranchised as returning citizens. John Calvin had a wonderful metaphor for our vision problem. Scripture, he said, provides the eyeglasses that we need. It is like a pair of spectacles by which we are enabled to see the world with clearer vision as God's creation and in light of God's plans and purposes. And the story of Scripture is not in black and white but in marvelous multicolored hues. It speaks of human diversity and color as a divine gift that is very, very good. By the power of God's Spirit, we are given real sight—able to perceive and embrace our multicolored hues as God's good gift.

After sharing some of these thoughts in the opening presentation, we broke into small groups and discussed two questions: (1) "Recount an experience that opened your mind and heart to the reality (the perspectives or sufferings) of the racial Other"; and (2) "How can we embody and proclaim Jesus' proclamation of good news—of the restoration of sight for the 'colorblind' (Luke 4:18)—in the community around us in D.C. today?" What follows is a small sampling of the feedback from that discussion:

When I came today, I thought . . .
> . . . It would be hard for a white church to host authentic conversation.
> . . . I'm glad I came, but it was hard.

Now I see . . .

> . . . the importance of whites speaking out against colorblindness.
>
> . . . through hearing others' stories, color has impacted people, limiting their opportunities to interact with others.
>
> . . . that I should stop being afraid of sharing my story.
>
> . . . we are becoming part of each other's lives. We enjoy the sober discussions and fellowship together.
>
> . . . that I look forward to understanding the theology of Martin Luther King Jr. My vision of what church can be is much bigger because of this experience.
>
> . . . the issues with our penal system related to race; we need to stop being colorblind regarding the impact of class.

Next time, I wish . . .

> . . . for more interaction/discussion with the other church members and to learn how to ask the tough questions.
>
> . . . we can tell more stories and focus on concrete efforts to eradicate poverty in D.C.

This concluding wish was addressed during our third conversation at the Mt. Lebanon Baptist Church. Rev. Lionel Edmonds led the discussion and chose to focus our attention on the absence of jobs for African Americans in Washington, D.C.—one of the wealthiest cities in the nation. Lionel introduced an acting troupe from his congregation who presented a role-play of a conversation between Martin Luther King Jr. and Malcolm X on race and poverty. The conversation ended with two black youths from the church demanding that the two civil rights icons focus their attention on jobs. The role-play was effective. It redirected our attention from our collective experience of racism toward concrete efforts to eliminate the effects of racism in poverty in Washington, D.C. Lionel then introduced Jahi Wise, an organizer for WIN whose work is focused on the creation of green jobs in D.C. I will say more about this venture in the following chapter on jobs. For now, let me just note that it was fascinating to observe the change in the dynamic of our conversation. Most of us came to the conversation expecting another dialogue on race, but what we ended up engaging was the reality of black rage at a key consequence of racism: the absence of economic opportunity.

Let me offer a few personal reflections on my experience of this dialogue on race and poverty. I grew up in St. Joseph, Missouri, a small city in the Midwest, at a time when the civil rights movement was underway, but the problems it addressed seemed far removed from life in my city. This perception, of course, was an illusion. Race was the subtext for much of what I experienced. My mother and father were musicians and both taught music in our home. My mother taught piano, and my father provided voice instruction. I remember a time when I traveled home for a visit with my mother in the mid 1980s, about eight years after my father had passed away. During that visit, my mother showed me the clipping of an article from the *Philadelphia Inquirer* about a black woman from St. Joe who had just become a noted celebrity in Philadelphia. She had segued a career of singing into a career as a prominent talk show host. In the article, she credited my father with teaching her voice and giving her the tools to express her musical talent. Mother was proud of the article. But when she put it down on the dining room table, she said something that I suppose I knew all along but something we had never discussed: she said, "Your father accepted blacks as students, but I never did." When I asked why, she replied, "I guess I was afraid." At that moment I recognized the racial dilemma of my life—both fear and inclusion, and right under the same roof! My hometown schools were integrated; the sports in which I participated were integrated; but we were still a segregated town, separated by our fears. And overcoming fear is not easy.

During our fourth and final conversation, Rev. Karen Brau of Luther Place invited us to a beautiful liturgical response to our collective study and conversation. We were asked to light a candle and to name out loud or in our hearts the nature of the dust we were shaking off our feet. The dust I named was "fear." Of course, fear that is ingrained, enculturated, entrenched is not easy to shake off. In May, when Professor James Cone joined us at the conclusion of our venture, he spoke of his motivation for writing the book we had studied together— what he called his "most painful book." He told us that he felt compelled to speak for his parents and all others who could not speak, for fear of retaliation, during the Jim Crow era. At that moment, it occurred to me that Jesus' words, "fear not," are addressed to all his disciples throughout the centuries—including his white and black ones in America— urging us to stay the course, to continue the journey along that arc of the universe that bends toward justice and reconciliation. For as Cone so eloquently puts it in the last words of his book: "No two people in America have had more violent and loving encounters than black and white people. . . . No gulf between blacks and whites is too great to overcome. . . . If America has the courage to confront the great sin and ongoing legacy of white supremacy with repentance and reparation there is hope 'beyond tragedy.'" May God grant us the courage to live into that challenge, trusting in the divine "power at work within us" that "is able to accomplish abundantly far more than all we can ask or imagine" (Eph. 3:20).

Practicum

Engaging a conversation about racism and poverty in America is one of the most difficult things that disciples of Jesus might find themselves compelled to do. In this practicum, I will be speaking as a white Christian because that is, after all, my social location, and I cannot and should not speak for others. My reflections in this chapter emerge from the context of my own congregation—a predominantly white congregation that has sought to address varied manifestations of institutional racism through its engagement in a range of social ministries with the homeless, the mentally ill, the unemployed, and struggling students in failing inner-city schools. The New York Avenue Church, in partnership with institutions like WIN, has been tackling such issues for years. Thus, though a predominantly European American church, we were already in relationship with African Americans and Latino/a Americans in our city. In my opinion, working interracial relationships are essential if we are to make any effective headway in our communities on issues of race and poverty. Indeed, if the New York Avenue church had not had a history of ministry in the city I'm not sure we could have engaged an authentic discussion about racism.

Thus, my first word of advice would be to attend to the suggestions provided in the practicum in chapter 1: engage your context, whatever it might be, giving special attention to the effects of institutional racism in your surrounding community. One way to get at this would be to conduct relational meetings with persons in your community who are racially or ethnically different from you: African American, Latino/a, Asian, Arab, European American, multiracial members of other religious congregations in your vicinity (churches, synagogues, or mosques). Relational meetings are described in chapters 1 and 2, and the only suggestion I would add here would be that when you tell your story, include something about your experience of racism. After conducting twenty or so one-on-one relational meetings, you might want to plan listening sessions (described in chapter 3) inviting those who have participated to join you (and inviting them to invite others). I would suggest a modest agenda for listening sessions—the sharing of stories is for the purpose of building relationships of trust and understanding. In my experience, it takes time to build relationships. Even though I had worked with Lionel Edmonds and Joe Daniels (and members of their congregations) within the WIN organization, it took time to build the authentic relationships necessary to ensure safe space for conversation about race. And even when we did finally engage the issue, it was an anxious venture.

Simultaneously, I would strongly urge facilitation of small group discussion within your congregation about racism. Through its educational ministries, many members of the New York Avenue congregation had engaged in some reading and conversation around the realities of race and poverty in advance of the tri-church venture, but I wish we had done even more. Indeed, after the initial foray into interracial conversations described in this chapter, I am proposing that we do more in-house conversation using resources like *White Like Me: Reflections on Race from a Privileged Son* by Tim Wise. This book is a very fine memoir that encourages white people to fight racism for their own sake. I also commend Tammerie Day's important new book, *Constructing Solidarity for a Liberative Ethic: Anti-Racism, Action, and Justice*, which evolved from her years of work in multicultural congregations. It is a book written from the perspective of a white Christian who believes that white Christians have a particular need to understand how their theologies have enabled racist practice. She points toward the critical need for white antiracist theology that subverts white privilege and what I would describe as its crucifying effects. In particular, she speaks of four "blockages" within the white Christian communion:

> . . . . one, the lack of attention to how our shared histories have created our divided present; two, the primacy of theologies that understand salvation as primarily about a life to come after our earthly lives are over, thereby obviating the need to address the death-in-life that is injustice here-and-now; three, the predominance among white people of a consciously or unconsciously white-privileging worldview; and four, the preference among white people to focus on racial reconciliation rather than the work of bringing about the concrete, material changes racial justice requires.[20]

With reference to Day's last point (the work of bringing about concrete change), by common consensus, our church-covenanting communities in D.C. have agreed as the next stage in our partnership together to take up the issue of institutional racism as it is manifested in economic inequality and the absence of living wage jobs. Among our goals is to help WIN hire another community organizer who will facilitate our work around issues of race, class, and economic empowerment. In other words, we plan to take concrete steps in addressing race and poverty in Washington D.C.

Chapter 7

Jobs in Urban Areas

I invite you to exercise your imagination and join me as I recollect an experience in the inner-city that proved to be a formative one for me. Imagine that it is a cool spring day and you are sitting on a blanket in a green meadow sipping a glass of wine, munching on crab cakes, and listening to the babble of a nearby brook. There's not a cloud in the sky, and a gentle breeze is blowing by. You could stay here forever. It is so wonderful— you must be dreaming. Baaaaaaaa! It is a dream, you quickly realize as the alarm clock jars you awake! You roll over and squint at the clock. It is 4:30 in the morning! Is this a joke or what? Who set the alarm for 4:30 a.m.? So you turn it off and roll over in bed and before you know it, you're almost back in the meadow. But then you remember that *you* set the alarm. You are meeting some of Baltimore's inner-city pastors downtown at 5:00 a.m. at a temporary employment agency. You are among the clergy leadership of the BUILD organization (Baltimoreans United in Leadership Development), and you agreed to go downtown to meet temporary workers and to learn what life is like in the world of the underemployed. But, oh, you were almost back in that meadow. . . . Maybe if you just keep your eyes closed for a second. No, ten minutes have passed—get up! The floor is so cold, and your knees are stiff.

As you enter the bathroom and look into the mirror, you come face-to-face with your own reflection, and it is not a pretty sight—your hair is greasy and in disarray and your eyes are puffy. Got to take a shower, you think, but there's no time. Besides, where you are headed, perhaps it is best to blend in. So you pull on your warmest sweatshirt, grab a coat and head downtown. But before you leave, you realize you better wear a hat since it is not going to be a good hair day. So which hat will it be? The one that says "Kool Jazz Festival"? No. How about the one that sports "Disney World"? No. There is always the dirty hat on the closet floor with sweat rings, the one that says: "Mack Trucks." Yeah, that's the one. Hat in place, you're off!

There's not much traffic on I-83 at this time in the morning; in fact, you're the only one on the road. Hey, this is not so bad. Maybe you ought to do this every morning. But then again, maybe not. You make your way to 421 N. Howard Street, to a place called TOPS, which stands for Temporary Overload Placement Service. And when you get there the first thing you see are vans— lots of vans—parked along the curb. All of them have the TOPS logo and a phone number painted on the side, and lots of men huddle along the curb where the vans are parked. Then you spot four BUILD pastors standing there, waiting for you. As you approach you notice that they're all wearing suits and ties, and that they are amused at your bedraggled appearance. One of them says: "So what are you trying to do, blend in?" And they laugh and laugh. Then one of them points out the food stains on the front of your sweat-shirt, and they think this is really funny too. Never mind, you may blend in after all.

You notice that you are standing next to a fast food joint called Mr. J's. It seems to be the main hangout for these underemployed folk. It is late in the fall of 1992, and even though you don't yet fully know what you are getting into, you are embarking on Baltimore's Living Wage Campaign. Jonathan Lange, one of the BUILD organizers, begins preparing you for the morning's event. He fills you in on what he knows about TOPS and what you are going to do. First of all, you learn that TOPS is an organization that contracts with Baltimore construction firms, housing complexes, and plants of all kinds; even the state of Maryland contracts with TOPS. But whatever the work site, the work is always the same—it is work that no one else wants to do: cleaning up construction sites, clearing trash, heavy lifting, and digging ditches. The kind of grunt work contractors wouldn't want to give to their full-time employees, so they contract with TOPS.

A contractor will pay TOPS anywhere from $10 to $14 an hour for each worker. This is a deal for the contractor, because they don't have to pay benefits, and they don't have to bother with part-time employees. TOPS then turns around and pays their workers minimum wage (which was $4.25 an hour in 1992). So it doesn't take much to figure out that somebody is making a lot of money off this deal, and it is not the workers. In fact, the contract includes a stipulation that the contractors themselves can't hire any of the TOPS temporary workers as full-time employees for up to a year beyond the time of the contract, or else they have to pay TOPS $500 per person. In this way, TOPS keeps people underemployed to ensure a steady pool of temporary workers. In addition, TOPS charges each worker for transportation, gloves if they need them, and lunch if they don't bring their own, and most don't. And all the work is on a first come, first served basis, which is why there is a crowd of folk assembled in the predawn hours. The doors open at 5:00 a.m., so if you want work, you'd better be there! At 5:00, TOPS distributes that day's job applications, and if a worker gets an application, he or she gets to work that day. The vans then take off at 6:00, so most of the workers who get an application go to Mr. J's to get some breakfast, because it is going be a long day. Jonathan then explains to you that you are going to go into Mr. J's too and talk with people to find out what it is like working with TOPS. He suggests that you shouldn't cover up what you're doing. Just tell them that you are with BUILD, he says—an organization of churches in the city—and that you've been noticing that the temporarily employed seem to be having a tough time making it, and you want to find out why. Jonathan even suggests that you might want to ask them if they are interested in forming their own temp work organization and see what they say.

With these instructions, the four of you make your way through the crowd at Mr. J's. You're uncomfortable, to say the least, especially since you're in the company of these guys in suits and ties. But at least you've got on a dirty sweatshirt and a hat that says "Mack Trucks." But soon you realize that you don't blend in any better than the "suits." Everyone is stealing glances in your direction, trying to figure out what you are doing there because it is clear you are out of place. What strikes you is that few of them are talking among themselves—they seem isolated. Some are reading newspapers, some are eating breakfast and sipping coffee, and a few are on the video arcade machines. They are in their 20s, 30s, 40s—a few look even older—and all of them look like they're ready for a hard day's work. Some wear the work dirt from the past few days on their clothes—dirt, perhaps, from the Ryland Home Townhouses going up in your neighborhood—homes they could never afford. But maybe you think to yourself, "Hey, somebody has got to clean up after the construction crews, and a bad job is better than no job at all, right?" You have a lot to learn about low-wage work in this country. Their hands look like they are accustomed to hard work, and you are suddenly very conscious of your own hands, which are soft and clean. You are quite clearly out of place: you are with the "suits!"

As you buy a cup of coffee, a young African American man in his early 20s walks through the door and says enthusiastically: "Hey, TOPS!" Few respond. And as he steps up to the counter right next to you, you notice that he is sizing you up. So you introduce yourself and tell him why you are here. You are nervous, so you say a bit more loudly than you intend: "Hi, I'm from BUILD—a church organization—and we're wondering whether any of you would be interested in forming your own temp work company!" You are way too loud. Several folk look in your direction. You wonder for a moment if the wrong person overheard you, remembering the time you visited a sister parish in El Salvador during their bloody civil war when a comment like that could get you murdered! But this is not El Salvador, it is inner-city Baltimore. The young man responds tersely: "Yeah. But just try organizing these folks!" And with that, he walks off.

You decide to try a more subtle approach. An older gentleman is sitting close to where you are standing, and he looks in your direction. He seems to have a slight smile on his face, so you sit down and introduce yourself. His name is Ripley, or Rip, as he likes to be called. Rip is a friendly man with kind eyes and an inviting smile, in his late fifties or sixties—not old enough for a social security check but too old for this kind of work. He is very open with you. He tells you that he has worked a variety of jobs in his life—as a waiter at a country club and in the laundry service of the Embassy Hotel in Hunt Valley (an exclusive part of Baltimore County). The most he has ever earned in his life was $6.00 an hour. And every time he has made enough money to live on, he's gotten laid off. But he has never been on public assistance; he has always worked, and he wants to work! And you think to yourself, here is someone who works and works hard, and he can barely pay the rent. Rip makes $138 a week, barely enough to keep him in a single room and to put a little food on the table. On Saturdays he goes to First and Franklin Street Presbyterian Church for breakfast because it saves on the food bill. You can't blame him for that. Finally, you ask him the question that plagues you the most: "How do you keep going?" Rip smiles, looks skyward, and says, "God helps me, God helps me!"

As Rip speaks, words of Jesus come to mind: "Come, you that are blessed by my Father, inherit the kingdom prepared for you from the foundation of the world; for I was hungry and you gave me food, I was thirsty and you gave me something to drink, I was a stranger and you welcomed me" (Matt. 25:35). Rip is a man who finds an occasional welcome in our church soup kitchens, but he has not been welcomed by society at large. And it is sobering, I think, to note that these words of Jesus, from his most vivid judgment tableau, are addressed not to individuals but to "the nations" who will be gathered before the throne and separated "as a shepherd separates the sheep from the goats." It is the nations who will be judged on the basis of whether or not they have extended welcome to the stranger. For Jesus also said, "Truly I tell you, just as you did it to one of the least of these who are members of my family, you did it to me" (Matt. 25:41). How could we as a society, as a nation, fail to see that Christ is truly present here at Mr. J's in the predawn hours of a Baltimore morning? Christ comes to us in every human being who crosses our paths, who haunts our conscience, who needs our attention.

Christ is warming himself on cold winter mornings over heating grates. He returns at the end of a hard workday to a lonely room, or maybe he has no room at all and grows old, unwanted and unkempt. Christ squats alone and afraid on every corner of our cities. You try not to look for fear that you'll be asked for spare change, but Christ is there.

You know, without a doubt, that you have encountered Christ in Rip as he filled out his application for yet another day's work. And as you make your way home to a warm shower and a hot breakfast, you are wondering—where will he work today, what will he do? Strangely enough, you went downtown this morning to bring the church to people in need and found that God was already there! Who knows, maybe you'll go back to TOPS again. Maybe you'll invite some people from your church to go with you. It's not like they will have anything else planned at 5 a.m. And how could you turn down an invitation to have morning coffee with the Lord?

The Living Wage Campaign

Ever since my encounter with Rip, community organizing and advocacy for jobs and living wages has played an important role in my experience of urban ministry. One of my proudest memories will always be my participation, and that of my congregation, with BUILD in the Living Wage Campaign in Baltimore where, in the mid-1990s, we fought for and helped pass the first living wage bill for city service workers in the country, elevating city service contracts from minimum wage to $9.00 an hour including benefits. This bill has since been replicated in more than thirty cities around the country, including New York City. A less known fact about the campaign is that we had much grander plans. We wanted to raise wages in the private sector as well as the public sector. Indeed, we had hopes of transforming Baltimore's crown jewel, the Inner Harbor—a historic seaport, tourist attraction, and landmark complex. These hopes were never fulfilled.

The massive redevelopment of Baltimore's Inner Harbor was advertised and promoted in election after election as an economic engine that would produce good jobs. But after three decades and more than two billion dollars of public subsidy, the Inner Harbor project had yielded few jobs that paid more than minimum wage, and many of those jobs had not even been fulltime. The enduring argument for this redevelopment project was the basic tenet that once workers entered the work force, they would move up the wage ladder— a vacuous promise, for the ladder turned out to be a very short one with little room at the top.[1] This same story, we learned, could be told in every U.S. city that pinned its future on convention business and the service industry. In fact, we finally realized that the only hope behind this economic scheme hinged on whether those in support of it were willing to attend one another's conventions! There were, to be sure, visitors in town for a convention who showed up for church services most Sundays, but they were not Baltimore's working poor. It was an economic plan that didn't really work because it did not work for everyone—certainly not for the janitors who sweep up after the conventioneers are gone or the housekeepers who clean up their messy hotel rooms.

The reality of the American service industry was captured for me in a memorable experience early in our campaign when we targeted the Inner Harbor hotels and the low wages they paid to their housekeepers. We had leveraged a meeting with the hotel managers that took place on the top floor of one of the hotels. The view out of the conference room window told the story of Baltimore's history. From that window, you could see the rivers that for almost three centuries have connected Baltimore's economy to the Chesapeake Bay, to the Atlantic, and to the historical economies of Europe, India, Asia, and other places. You could also see the now-defunct warehouses and factories of Baltimore's economic past, which once housed one of the largest garment and railroad industries in the nation. These buildings now house the Baltimore Orioles's office complex, the ESPN Zone, and Starbucks Coffee, among other businesses. We were meeting with the hotel managers for a simple reason: to advocate on behalf of their housekeepers. Our research told us those housekeepers made $5.10 an hour in Baltimore City, $7.00 in Baltimore County, and much more than that in Howard County and neighboring Washington, D.C. We presented this information and more, along with an idea: if everyone who came to Baltimore for a convention or vacation were asked to pay a single dollar more per night for a room, you could inch a housekeeper's salary toward the living wage.

Well, the managers were respectful, but it was not hard to tell that they thought we were crazy. In a prior religious era, they might have been inclined to burn us at the stake for heresy! Indeed, one of them suggested as much when he pronounced (with an air of confidence) that "there is an 'invisible hand' that guides the rate of wages paid in Baltimore City and elsewhere in this country, and we dare not mess with it." Now I confess that I was disconcerted by his statement, an obvious allusion to Adam Smith's dogma of modern capitalism. But one minister among us kept his poise. Without missing a beat, he responded, "I, too, believe in an 'invisible hand,' one that cares deeply for the least well-off in our city. And working for or against the invisible hand of God, who cares deeply for the poor, is a flesh and blood hand, and that flesh and blood hand belongs to you!" While a bit stunned by the minister's bravado, the hotel manager was unmoved, no doubt because he believed that capitalist dogma was on his side. Needless to say, our negotiations that day went nowhere. In fact, we decided to "walk out" of the meeting that day because the hotel managers maintained a strident stand based on the dogma of the "invisible hand."

A few years ago I read Arthur Herman's fascinating book *How the Scots Invented the Modern World.* According to Herman, there are plenty of myths about the Scottish philosopher Adam Smith, and one of those myths is about the "invisible hand." The notion that Adam Smith believed that the prices and availability of goods and services, and the wages paid to those who provide them, is perfectly regulated by an "invisible hand" turns out to be a fiction. Smith's point was not that the market system was without flaw but rather that its "invisible hand" was preferable to reliance on the will of the politicians and monarchs of his day who cared for little more than their own irrational "passions and whims."[2] Another myth about Adam Smith is that his philosophy was basically an argument for big business. Wrong. In fact, Smith paints a very unflattering picture of the businessman for whom greed and profit is the only end. Moreover, Smith warned against the degradation of the worker that could result from preoccupation with profit and loss. Indeed, he argued that "[T]hrough capitalism we gain, but we also lose. The loss, Smith felt, was felt most among the lowest classes."[3]

Adam Smith may not have been an apologist for big business, but he wasn't antibusiness either. Neither am I. While at one time I might have inclined in that direction, my mind changed in the mid-1990s when I was invited to team-teach a business ethics course at the Johns Hopkins School of Continuing Studies. I was asked to teach the course not because I knew a lot about business or economics but because a close friend of mine who did know a lot about business needed someone with a degree in ethics to team-teach with him, and I was the only one he knew who fit that description. I told him that I tended to regard the juxtaposition of business and ethics as oxymoronic, and he said that he hoped to prove me wrong. Over the course of several years of teaching together, he did just that. What I learned from him is that there are many good people in business who face heart-rending decisions on a regular basis and genuinely want to do the right thing in difficult circumstances.

I seldom expressed my Christian convictions in class (Johns Hopkins is, after all, a secular university). Yet privately I ruminated upon them and upon the implications of this course in business ethics for my work, and that of my congregation, in the living wage campaign. And I became convinced that, from a Christian standpoint, there is no perfectible economic system.

The lens of suspicion (which I discussed in chapter 1) calls all economies to account for their ill treatment of the poor and the outcast. The New Testament book of James articulates an appropriate Christian posture toward economics when it defines true religion in this manner: "Religion that is pure and undefiled before God, the Father, is this: to care for orphans and widows in their distress, and to keep oneself unstained by the world" (Jas. 1:27). Throughout both the Old Testament and the New, widows and orphans are shorthand symbols of the marginalized. This text thus suggests that the measure of authentic religion is whether or not our attention is focused on the least well off. Only as we take them into account can we begin to discern how to reform an economic system.

I was aided in my reflections by one of the textbooks we used for our course, Robert Solomon's *Ethics and Excellence: Cooperation and Integrity in Business*. In this book, Solomon argues that the first principle of business ethics is not the profit motive, but rather "that the corporation is itself a citizen, a member of the larger community."[4] He debunks the spurious notion that corporations are autonomous, independent creatures; they, like individuals, are integral to the communities out of which they come and in which they reside. Moreover, Solomon says,

> So, too, what drives the corporation is not some mysterious abstraction called "the profit motive" (which is highly implausible even as a personal motive, but utter nonsense when applied to a bureaucracy). It is the collective will and ambitions of its employees. . . . Employees of a corporation do what they must do to fit in, to perform their jobs and to earn the respect of others and self-respect. They want to prove their value in their jobs . . . they want to feel good about themselves. . . . And, of course, they want to bring home a paycheck.[5]

It seems to me that Solomon's notion of the corporation as a "citizen" whose employees are integral to the whole corresponds to Christian covenant responsibility, which entails the love of neighbor mandated by the Great Commandment. Indeed, Solomon's description is in many respects a secular equivalent to our Christian calling and vocation. These perspectives were helpful to me as we engaged in the living wage campaign, because Solomon's observations are a trenchant critique of many temp work organizations and many hotels where the housekeepers work for their poverty.

Not long after meeting with the hotel managers, BUILD decided to shift the course of the campaign. This decision came after a portentous meeting with Kurt Schmoke, the Mayor of Baltimore at the time. It is important to know something about the background of this meeting. Kurt Schmoke was a star graduate of the Baltimore City public school system and went on to become a graduate of Yale University and Harvard Law School and a Rhodes Scholar. In short, he is a very intelligent man. But as mayor of Baltimore he was often overly reflective and indecisive. Though concerned for the well-being of his hometown, he seemed to be trapped under the thumb of the Baltimore elite who could make or break him as mayor. Schmoke initially supported BUILD's living wage efforts and made a few public comments to that effect, until Baltimore's business community began to hammer him. Even the *Baltimore Sun*'s editorial staff opined that BUILD's living wage campaign was giving Baltimore a "black eye" and that if a city living wage bill was passed, Baltimore would no longer be attractive for businesses. The net result would be job loss, not gain.

Some of the members of my congregation shared the concerns of the *Sun*'s editorial staff and were wondering the same thing and raised questions about our church's involvement in the living wage campaign. Some of them actively supported the Inner Harbor redevelopment project because of the promise of jobs; even after that promise fell flat, they continued to believe in the canon principle that minimum wage work was an anchor in the workplace and could lead to a better life. Perhaps there was some truth to this principle when the minimum wage law was passed in the 1960s, but by the 1990s this could no longer be argued convincingly. It was increasingly clear that minimum wage labor could not sustain worker's lives. The notion that it could better one's state in life is what Beth Schulman and Paul Osterman refer to as the "Horatio Alger" myth, and they give plenty of statistics that explode it.[6] As part of my effort to engage folk, I conducted relational meetings and listening sessions with members of my church. Some minds were changed by their involvement in the campaign. Others decided to "put up" with BUILD's activities, concluding that they would just let this be "Roger's thing." Though I don't like conflict (the truth is, I hate it, as most of us do!), one thing I've learned is that if there is no tension, neither people nor churches grow, so I've tried my best to embrace it.

On the day of our fateful meeting with Kurt Schmoke, the BUILD leadership (which included several low-income workers) was waiting outside his office while he concluded a prior meeting. It wasn't long before the doors of his office opened and twelve hotel managers, along with their area supervisors, walked out. Of course, they recognized many of us from our previous meeting, and they conveyed a perceptible air of confidence as they passed and shook our hands! Later, in our meeting with Schmoke, when pressed by one of the workers to actively promote a living wage bill for Baltimore, he responded, "You all are revolutionaries, but I have to be the mayor of the whole city." By this he meant that he had withdrawn his support of our initiative and that he stood with the business community.

After this meeting, we knew what we had to do. Upcoming elections were on the near horizon, and thus we had leverage that could be deployed on Schmoke and the Baltimore City Council on the matter of city service contract jobs. Thus we shifted our focus from the private sector to public sector jobs, pressing for living wage legislation on that front. After much groundwork, and with the help of a key ally, the Baltimore City Council President Mary Pat Clarke, Schmoke, and the rest of City Council finally gave into our demands at "an action" (that is, at a large public gathering called for the purpose of pressuring public officials for accountability) at which we turned out more than two thousand BUILD church members and low-wage workers. Ironically, this gathering was held in the grand ballrooms of one of the city convention center hotels! Thus, with the support of the mayor and council, in 1994 the city council passed the first living wage bill for city-service contracts in the country: the bill raised service contract wage from $4.25 up to $9.00 per hour with benefits. It was a great victory! But sadly, we never had another meeting with the hotel managers and never found traction for a living wage in the private sector.

One moment during that campaign will forever be imprinted on my memory and gives me goose bumps to this day. It happened at a BUILD meeting attended by approximately five hundred people—both low-wage workers and BUILD church folk—during which we strategized about our next move. Some of the workers shared that they had been threatened with job loss if they continued to work with BUILD on this campaign. The late Rev. Vernon Dobson, one of the founding members of BUILD who was the longtime pastor of Union Baptist Church and one of Baltimore's civil rights heroes, stood to encourage the workers to stay the course. It seemed me that fire was coming out of his fingers as he pledged to the workers, "If anyone threatens you again, all of the pastors in this room, all of the churches in BUILD represented here today, will stand with you; we will support you so that they can't fire you, and we will make sure that they don't threaten you again. And we will do that because you are all children of God!" I knew then and there that no matter what tensions we might be facing in the city (and in our own congregations) over our advocacy for a living wage, there was a higher calling. For me it was a calling to steadfastly stand with Rip and his coworkers and to continue to work for the day when every one of God's children has a job that can create and sustain a life.

Vocation and the Politics of Resurrection

As a congregation, in partnership with others, engages in public advocacy for jobs and living wages, it is crucial to provide theological grounding for such ministry. In my Reformed theological heritage, work is an expression of our spirituality and Christian discipleship and should help us realize our chief end as human creatures: "to glorify God, and to enjoy God forever."[7] In fact, Reformed theologian Doug Ottati claims that "in authentic practice of Reformed piety, worship and work are inextricably connected."[8] This is what he says about work, the occupations in which we engage:

> Properly understood and properly reformed, the ordinary is spiritual and the spiritual is ordinary. The spiritual sanctifies the ordinary and the ordinary disciplines the spiritual. There is no such thing as a profane or merely secular order from which God is absent, and in which God is not to be served. . . . Genuine faithfulness and the good life, then, are not defined by an exalted occupation, or activity, but by the way in which one lives in any and all occupations, offices, and activities. This is really as anti-elitist a notion of the Christian life as it first appears, one that contains the seeds for a discipleship of equals.[9]

Ottati thus commends a "vigilant . . . even suspicious" attitude toward organizations and their practices when they fail to contribute to the common good.[10]

So what are Christians to do when unjust wage practices are deforming human lives in the community around them? Here again Ottati's four prepositions for the church's involvement in the world can guide us. If the church is *in* the world, never giving up on God's good creation; *with* the world, confessing our common faults and sins; and *against* the world, bearing prophetic witness for the sake of the crucified and resurrected creation; then the church is also *for* the world because it is a community of hope. Given these four postures toward the world, the church must take a stand in the world with "crucified" workers in our communities and stand against realities that deform their lives. There is no denying that the church, through the ages, has not always distinguished itself in this regard.

A stinging and enduring critique of Christianity was articulated by Karl Marx, for example, when he spoke of religion as the "opiate of the people." Whatever one's assessment of Marxism and its flawed history, one of its abiding legacies is its trenchant critique of religion that promotes social passivity and blesses an unjust social order. There is a scene from the 1981 epic film *Reds* that gave expression to this critique—the scene in which Louise Bryant (an American woman sympathetic with the Bolshevist revolution in Russia) is being questioned by Senator Lee Overman, who in 1918 established a Senate committee to investigate Communist elements in American society. When the Senator asks Bryant whether she is a Christian, Bryant answers, "I believe in the teachings of Jesus." The Senator replies, "Are there no God-fearing Christians among the Bolsheviks?" Answer: "Does one have to be God-fearing and Christian to be decent? Senator, the Bolsheviks believe that it is religion, particularly Christianity, that's kept the Russian people back for so many centuries."[11] Christianity, of course, has not been the only religion in human history to thwart social progress and bless the status quo, but given its dominance in the history of Western and Eastern countries, it (and we) are particularly culpable. And if there is one tenet of Christian belief that has been especially susceptible to use as an opiate (that is, as a belief that renders people passive in the face injustice), it is the Christian belief in the afterlife or resurrection. Resurrection can be (and frequently has been) misconstrued as the belief that suffering in the present can be tolerated because of the hope for a better life "in the sweet by and by."

Ironically, the origins of the Christian notion of resurrection had politically subversive roots. Theologian Ted Jennings helpfully traces the political roots of resurrection to Judaism during the period of the Maccabean revolt against the Seleucid king Antiochus IV Epiphanes (ruled 175–164 BCE), two centuries before Christ. Antiochus aggressively promoted a trend toward Hellenization, assumed the power to appoint high priests in Jerusalem and ultimately issued decrees forbidding Jewish religious practices. The Maccabean resistance to this tyranny led to the execution of many martyrs who maintained loyalty to the faith. Subsequently, belief in the resurrection of the executed emerged as an insurrectionist protest against the fate of the slain (Dan. 12:2–3). As Jennings puts it, "The resurrection of the executed is the hope for divine justice that overthrows the dominion of the tyrant."[12] And this belief endured into the New Testament era. According to Jennings, the New Testament developed the politics of resurrection and came to believe that "in the resurrection of Jesus the principalities and powers of the world are already judged and condemned as rebels against the rule of God."[13] In chapter 3, we noted that the book of Revelation presents the resurrected Christ as calling on the church to "pick a fight" with Roman tyranny. Thus, it is much too simplistic to equate Christian teaching of "resurrection" with passivity in the face of injustice. In much of Christian tradition, resurrection has had decidedly political implications. So a political reading of resurrection counters the charge that Christianity aims to render people passive in the face of injustice.

Still, while critical of Marx's political philosophy or critique of religion, Christians might well share his outrage at the conditions of the working class during the industrial revolution. Indeed, on this point liberation theologians have likened Marx to the ancient prophets of Israel who condemned the exploitation of the poor. Management of low-income work has come a long way since the days of Marx: workplace laws and regulations, worker rights, and childhood labor laws have significantly improved working conditions, in America at least. Even so, a full quarter of working adults in the United States today serve in jobs that pay wages that hover at the poverty level, and their prospects for finding better work are dismal.

Thus, the message of the risen Christ to the church in the book of Revelation still holds relevance for us today: "pick a fight!" And advocating for jobs and living wages that will sustain life is a fight—indeed, a ministry—well worth joining. As Osterman and Shulman remind us, the "myth of upward mobility is just that . . . a myth." And they conclude their book on jobs in America by reminding us also that the long-term cost of low-income work on families, communities and the body politic is real: "In a country as rich as ours, with as great a potential as our country has, it is just unacceptable that a parent cannot attend a school conference because it would mean lost pay, that a mother ignores her diabetes because the trade-off is school books for her children, that a nursing assistant is unable to afford a safe place to live."[14] The authors point to two contrasting notions of democracy at work in America: in one, the goal of the political and economic system is to maximize the well-being of the consumer by freeing firms to drive prices to the lowest level (achieved by the driving of wages to the lowest level); while the other has the objective of enabling citizens to participate fully in democratic deliberation—to be full citizens, which is not a possibility for economically marginal people.[15]

The truth of the matter is that good work is in everyone's interests: it's a win-win for employers who need stability and efficiency in the workplace; for families who need to clothe, feed, and safely house their children; for the city that needs the tax revenue; and for those of us considered "middle class" as well, because financial exigencies can befall us all, leaving us no other options except low-income work. Good work is good for all and serves our common life together just as bad work is harmful for all and erodes the common good. Indeed, for Christians, good work is sign of resurrection wherein the justice and reconciliation of the cruciform God brings life from the death of oppressive work and its crucifying effects on us all: because when one is crucified, we are all crucified; and when one is resurrected, we are all resurrected. As Martin Luther King Jr. so eloquently put it, "We are caught in an inescapable network of mutuality, tied in a single garment of destiny. Whatever affects one directly, affects all indirectly."

At the turn of the century, you couldn't find a more basic metaphor for interdependency and interrelatedness than baseball. In fact, for many in the social gospel movement in the early twentieth century, the game served as an illustration of how Americans from different classes and ethnic backgrounds could work cooperatively to build a better society. Ballparks were built as monuments to middle- and working-class virtue. For many, baseball was the perfect embodiment of teamwork, and the essence of Christianity could be taught to those who grasped the cooperative aspects of the game. But eventually, the greed of the owners evoked ongoing tensions with players, and the escalation of player salaries ensued—with the result that baseball now has become a mirror of society, as has virtually every other professional sport. Now the only sacrifice in baseball is a bunt or a fly ball out that scores a run, for which the player gets credit. In his book on baseball and religion, Chris Evans contends that what is missing from baseball is an embrace of Martin Luther King's dream of the beloved community in which all Americans are tied together within an interconnected fabric of common destiny. [16] It is missing from our common life as well.

Crucifixion and Prodigals

As a congregation takes a stand in the world with "crucified" workers in their community and against realities that oppress them, it does so as a community of hope and resurrection. As I have noted before, the interpretive lens by which we view the world is twofold and includes both suspicion and grace. The lens of suspicion asks the question, Who or what is being crucified? The lens of grace asks the question, Where is God bringing life, or resurrection and sanctification, out of the death-tending idolatries of the world? Our vision, however, is also deeply influenced by our "social location," which affects not only what we see but also the questions we think to ask. Thus the lens of suspicion and grace must be brought to bear on our own lives as well.

The impact of social location on our perception is underscored by a fascinating experiment that biblical scholar Mark Allan Powell once conducted on readings of the parable of the Prodigal Son. It was a simple experiment but a revealing one, conducted first with seminarians in America and later with seminarians in Russia and Tanzania. He asked them to read the parable and then to close their Bibles and recount it from memory to a partner. What struck him most were the very different ways in which these three groups accounted for the downfall of the prodigal in their recitations of the biblical story:"A few days later the younger son gathered all he had and traveled to a distant country, and there he squandered his property in dissolute living. When he had spent everything, a severe famine took place throughout that country, and he began to be in need" (Luke 15:13–14). What accounted for the prodigal's undoing? In their recollections of this moment in the story, 100 percent of the American seminarians explained that the prodigal squandered his property in dissolute living but barely mentioned the famine. By contrast, the Russian seminarians, residents of St. Petersburg, emphasized the famine, but few mentioned the prodigal's squandering of his property. Powell didn't have to look far for the reason. In 1941, the German army laid siege to the city of St. Petersburg and subjected its inhabitants to a nine-hundred-day famine. During that time, 670,000 people died of starvation and exposure. For their descendants, the mention of famine would never be an extraneous detail, because to this day in St. Petersburg social issues are considered through the lens of an important question: What if there is not enough food? Moreover, in a socialist state, the sin is self-sufficiency. The prodigal's sin was that he wanted to make it in the world on his own, but in a world where famines can occur only a fool would want to be alone. For Americans, however, the great sin was wasting money. In a capitalist society, it is a very bad thing to squander one's inheritance.

So what about the Tanzanians of East Africa? Powell was intrigued to find yet another different emphasis in their telling of the prodigal's downfall. Eighty percent of the Tanzanian seminarians focused on the fact that during the famine, *no one gave the prodigal anything to eat.* Hospitality plays a critically important role in African society, and thus their attention was captured by a detail noted in a later verse in the story: "He would gladly have filled himself with the pods that the pigs were eating; and no one gave him anything" (15:16).[17]

Clearly our social locations and circumstances affect what we see and even the questions we are inclined to ask. Our interpretation of the world is always perspectival. Moreover, hearing and engaging the perspectives of others can enable us to see something we might otherwise have missed. Powell's fascinating experiment got me thinking: how might Rip and other underemployed or low-wage workers hear the parable of the Prodigal Son? I suspected that they would draw our attention to an altogether different emphasis in the story: "So he went and hired himself out to one of the citizens of that country, who sent him to his fields to feed the pigs" (15:15). This facet of the story might be overlooked by some, but others might find it the critical part of the story. In the social context of the story, feeding pigs was perhaps the most demeaning work that a Jewish boy would have to resort to. Moreover, Jesus tells us, *"He would gladly have filled himself with the pods that the pigs were eating; and no one gave him anything"* (15:16). In other words, it was nasty, degrading work, and it didn't even earn him enough to feed himself properly. Luke's parable now brings to mind for me the working poor in Baltimore who show up at soup kitchens for meals and the working homeless folk in Washington, D.C., who show up at New York Avenue's Radcliffe Room ministry on Sunday mornings because they don't make enough to either feed or house themselves. Is not the plight of these people strikingly akin to that of the prodigal son in Luke's story? I would hesitate to use the word "prodigal" to describe today's low-income workers, but neither would I want to claim sainthood for them. Indeed, the reality of low-income work, of wages that cannot sustain a life, can make prodigals of us all.

Given these realities, the urban church could take up no more worthy ministry than that of advocating and organizing for good jobs that pay a living wage. Recent studies have shown that the economic disparity between whites and blacks in this country has only worsened since the economic meltdown of 2008. Indeed, economist Tom Shapiro contends that if this is not addressed, and addressed quickly, it will create a permanent underclass of black people in America.[18]

I can't help but wonder how Luke's parable would have unfolded if the prodigal had found a good paying job that earned a living wage with benefits—a job that wasn't degrading, that helped him put food on the table. And suppose he got married, had a family, and created a life for himself? Would that ruin the happy ending of the prodigal's homecoming? No father running down the road to embrace his lost child, forgiveness and all that. Perhaps it is all a matter of perspective. One thing I can tell you is that as I was plodding my way through graduate school, my mother spent the whole time wondering (and sometimes even asking), *"When* are you going to get a job?" And when I was finally ordained as a Presbyterian minister, with a real job providing a salary with benefits, she embraced me and killed the fatted calf, and we had a feast, and she said to me, "all is forgiven." I thank God for good work to do, the work of ministry, which has a role to play in ensuring that others, too, can find worthy labor with living wages that restore them to the dignity for which they were created and can hear the divine voice proclaiming: *this child of mine was dead and is alive again; (s)he was lost and has been found!* (cf. Luke 15:32).

Green Jobs

The possibilities for church-based advocacy on behalf of jobs and living wage work will vary from place to place, depending on local needs and challenges.

But perhaps further examples might prompt reflection on the kinds of projects that might be engaged. As I write these words, WIN (the Washington Interfaith Network) has launched an initiative on green jobs that could prove to be as consequential as the living wage campaign in Baltimore. Here is the background: If you live in a city just about anywhere in the United States, check your water bill and you are likely to find that you are also paying to rectify the problem of storm water runoff. When it rains, millions of gallons of water run into our antiquated storm water systems, causing flooding and the overflow of untreated sewage and other pollutants into local rivers. In 2005, D.C. Water reached a legal agreement with the Environmental Protection Agency to reduce these overflows by 96 percent by 2025. Thus, D.C. Water initiated a 2.6 billion dollar Clean Rivers Project to achieve this goal, and our current water bills include a surcharge to cover the cost of this initiative. In other words, D.C. residents are paying to correct the storm water problem. So shouldn't we have something to say about how this problem might be best resolved—and about the kinds of jobs that could be created to solve it? We think so.

There are two alternative ways to contain storm water. One strategy would be to build huge containers by using large tunnel building machines, but this produces few jobs. Those it does produce tend not to stay in the area but rather move on to the next tunnel-building project in another city. The other strategy is green and ecologically advisable because it uses rain gardens, pervious pavement, and green roofs as a natural means by which to absorb water and replenish aquifers. It also produces good jobs; as many as four thousand are projected for the D.C. area alone. When you replicate these numbers in every major city in the country, we're talking about the possibility of creating millions of jobs. WIN and its member congregations obviously think the latter strategy is the way to go. In fact, a recent study suggested that the only problem with the green route is that green infrastructure needs to be maintained.[19] If so, we figure that is a good problem to have, because the jobs created to build the green infrastructure can also then be employed to maintain it. In other words, these jobs could sustain folk with a living wage for a long time!

There are, of course, obstacles that will need to be addressed. These jobs do not create themselves. City agencies will face substantial hurdles implementing green infrastructure and the city's residents will need to buy in to the plan if it is to work. So what is needed is an organized base of water consumers, job seekers, business people, and environmentalists to hold the city and water company accountable for hiring and training workers for these jobs. Organizing these disparate groups will not be easy, but the way we see it, such a strategy will benefit almost everyone affected.

Moreover, the jobs that would be created would reverse the longstanding trend of replacing humans with machines. Over the last century, technological advances have replaced people with machines at a staggering rate. As Jeremy Rifkin points out, "More than 800 million human beings are now unemployed or underemployed in the world. That figure is likely to rise sharply between now and the end of the century as millions of new entrants into the workforce find themselves without jobs, many victims of a technology revolution that is fast replacing human beings in virtually every sector and industry of the global economy."[20] Green jobs in the storm-water industry, however, could be one of the few exceptions to this global trend. The green solution to the problem of storm-water runoff requires workers more than machines and thus has a critical social, ecological, environmentally-responsible impact.

The way WIN sees it, the green job initiative is a win-win proposition. The water consumer is going to have to pay for rectifying the storm-water problem one way or another, so why not train and employ people for good and important work that benefits the common good?[21] And the way I see it, the reasons the church might want to advocate for such an alternative are compelling. Many of the folk served by our homeless ministries are underemployed and thus work for their poverty, and this must end. There is no question that living wage jobs would represent a preferable alternative to soup kitchens! Thus, the New York Avenue church will continue to work and pray for the day when our breakfast program for the homeless closes down because it is no longer needed!

Walmart

Some congregations within Washington, D.C., have recently also discerned another front on which advocacy on behalf of jobs and living wages has been called for. In the summer of 2013, the city found itself in the midst of a heated (no pun intended) debate involving Walmart, the largest corporate employer in the world. In July, the city council approved a living wage bill that would require large retailers such as Walmart to pay their employees 50 percent over the minimum wage ($12.50 an hour). This decision came a day after Walmart warned in an editorial in the *Washington Post* that the law would jeopardize its plans to open stores in the city (where, currently, there are none). The mayor of D.C. also has a vital stake in this issue. Mayor Vincent Grey has supported Walmart's entry into the city, arguing that the company would bring badly needed jobs and retail stores to neighborhoods in need of both. Gray has made a particular push to have Walmart anchor a development in the Skyland Town Center, near his home.

The Skyland Shopping Center in southwest D.C. deserves special comment. A *Washington Post* description of the current shopping center reported that it is, to say the least, bleak. In July 2013, most of the shops were shuttered and windows broken, and someone had dragged a mattress into the closed post office. A good-bye note was posted on the window of a recently closed beauty supply store reading, "Thank you for 38 years." Moreover, the Skyland area of D.C. has become a food desert, which means that its residents have to travel a good distance into neighboring Prince George's County to find a decent grocery store. Kevin Brown, a jobless resident of the Skyland area, was angry that Walmart was not willing to pay higher wages. Nonetheless he was reported as saying, "Something is better than nothing, then work your way up."[22] Yet it is common knowledge that you can't afford to live in Skyland on $8.25 an hour (D.C.'s current minimum wage, which is $1.00 above the national minimum). The cheapest apartments in the area rent for almost $800 per month, so in order to create a life in Skyland on a minimum wage, you would have to work at least 80 hours per week.[23]

The debate on this issue assumed such a high profile that it made the *PBS News Hour.* On the news program, two pundits argued their cases for and against a living wage—and, in particular, on the question of whether it would have an effect on the number of jobs produced. One pundit pointed to studies suggesting that increased wages have no adverse effect on employment, while the other claimed the opposite, insisting that increased wages cause unemployment. They went back and forth, citing study after study.[24] It was, for me, a déjà vu moment that recalled my experience in Baltimore, where the living wage in fact had no adverse effect on unemployment figures. People continue to debate this matter, but whatever the case may be, journalist Matt Miller has documented that the United States ranks near the bottom of industrialized countries when it comes to minimum to median wages. He points out that "in Australia, the minimum wage now tops $15.00 and unemployment is 5.4 percent." Moreover, plenty of economic thinkers (not just progressive ones but also conservatives and libertarians) are currently highlighting the urgency of closing our income gap so that all Americans can earn a decent wage.[25]

As I eavesdrop on such debates among pundits, I find myself wondering: When will people living in poverty be included in this discussion so that we can begin to learn what it is actually like to try to live on a minimum wage? The debate is an elitist abstraction until their voices are included. Low-wage workers need to be part of the decision-making process as we figure out how to move toward a living wage. The church can play a role in ensuring that this happens. It can covenant with such workers in its community and insist that they have a place at the table. A table is, after all, at the heart of the church's life — one at which all are welcome. And did not the apostle Paul's instruction on Communion practice to the church at Corinth include the principle of "equal food for all at the center of communion"?[26] Liturgical scholar Paul Galbreath persuasively argues that what we do at the Lord's Table is a pattern for "our lives and our actions."[27] This vision can impel us to work without ceasing for the day when all God's children are welcome at the table. A place at God's table is extended to all, and we should not rest until this comes to pass.

But until that day comes, this is the situation with which we are faced: we live in a consumer society that continues to favor low prices over decent jobs at fair wages. The American myth of advancement, the notion that you can pull yourself up by your own bootstraps, continues to prevail. Pundits continue to argue while the working poor die on the streets. Yet in spite of this, the church is called to remain hopeful and vigilant, because, as Doug Ottati so eloquently puts it,

> The arc of the universe is God's arc, and this arc, although we cannot always make out its curvature, bends toward God's universal commonwealth, kingdom, or city. Finally, not without confessing sins, not apart from judgments, prophetic criticisms, chastening defeats, and passionate sufferings, reforming piety supports a truly cosmic optimism. The God of grace and glory, the power of goodness made perfect in weakness, is greater than the power of evil. . . . This is why the church is *for* the world.[28]

So let's get back to the trenches of urban ministry to participate in the future that God has in mind for us as it struggles toward realization now.

Practicum

This chapter easily could have focused on other urban issues besides jobs. Urban areas struggle with a critical triumvirate of issues that are inextricably intertwined, and addressing any one of them impacts the others. This triumvirate consists of jobs, education, and low-income housing. An entire chapter could have been addressed to each of these critical issues, with attention to their interrelationships. Consider, for example, the following interconnections: low-income housing depends on a good paying job that will create leverage for a loan with which to buy a home; a home is an anchor in a neighborhood and helps to create a stable environment in which schools can thrive; schools are critical if youth are to be educated and trained for the workplace and to achieve a position to contribute to the common good; and a good paying job is critical in order for parents to find the free time in which to exercise citizenship in a community and to contribute to their children's lives. This triumvirate of issues corresponds, in my view, to the aspects of the Great Commandment symbolized by the three-legged stool: one leg for the heart (home), one leg for the mind (public education), and one leg for the will (work). The congregations that I have served, and the affiliate organizations such as BUILD and WIN with which we have partnered, have attempted to work in all three arenas, but it isn't an easy balancing act. All three arenas present problems and possibilities that a congregation may wish to engage in its ministry to the community around it. Jobs and wages have been the focus of this particular chapter, but I want to acknowledge that when we talk about jobs other issues are also at stake.

As you discern possibilities for ministry within your own community, consider the following questions and suggestions as resources for individual or collective reflection:

1. Do you know of any temp work organizations in your city or neighborhood? Do you know people who do temp work and what they are paid? If the answer to these questions is no, then you may want to investigate these matters. If there are construction workers or managers in your church, there may be things you can learn from them about temp workers in their worksites. How might you make the acquaintance of temp workers? Make acquaintances among temp workers and ask them about their lives. Do a relational meeting with them.

2. You may wish to engage in group Bible study of Matthew 25:31–46. Note the checklist of items that forms the basis on which "the nations" are judged—it is repeated four times! Reflect together on how this passage relates to you individually, to your congregation, and to our nation.

3. As you go about your daily activities, pay attention to people who may be engaged in service on your behalf: the people cleaning your workspaces or the bathrooms, emptying the trash or collecting the garbage, sweeping the streets, staffing Starbucks or McDonalds or the department store. What can you learn about their wages? (Some of this information is available on the Internet.) If you are bold (and I would encourage you to be so) and circumstances allow (e.g., if you are talking alone with a salesperson or you see a street cleaner by himself or herself), ask a few simple questions like: Do you mind my

asking how you like your job? What is the pay scale for this kind of work? In other words, become aware of how people feel about their work and their pay. If you are staying in a hotel, you might have an opportunity to speak with housekeepers. Be discrete and make it a short conversation so as not to distract them from their work. (I spent an afternoon walking through a Baltimore Inner Harbor hotel asking housekeepers about their jobs. I found them to be quite open in talking with me, and I learned a great deal.)

4. You may want to reflect on the "invisible hand" of the marketplace. See what opinions come up if you broach the subject. Revisit Arthur Herman's reflections on prevailing myths about Adam Smith and Robert Solomon's notion of the purpose of a corporation. How do their observations correspond to your understanding of Christian values?

5. Revisit Doug Ottati's understanding of worship and work. What do you think of his observations? How does work reflect—or fail to reflect—the glory of God in your life or in the lives of those around you?

6. What do you think of Marx's axiom that religion is the "opiate of the people"? What new insights did you gain from the discussion of political understandings of resurrection in this chapter? How might they sensitize us to the plight of the working poor?

7. Consider Osterman and Shulman's discussion of the myth of upward mobility: "In a country as rich as ours… it is just unacceptable that a parent cannot attend a school conference because it would mean lost pay, that a mother ignores her diabetes because the trade-off is school books for her children, that a nursing assistant is unable to afford a safe place to live."[29] The authors point to two contrasting notions of democracy: in one, the goal is to maximize the well-being of the consumer, and in the other it is to enable citizens to fully participate in democracy. They conclude that the latter is not possible for economically marginal people. What strikes you about these observations? What questions do they raise for you?

8. What insights did you gain from the discussion of varied perspectives on the Prodigal Son's downfall? What did you think of the perspective that a low-income worker might have on this story?

9. Examine your water bills to see if you are paying for rectification of the issue of storm water runoff. If so, do you know how your local water company is addressing this problem? Are there environmentalists or landscape architects in your church or community who might have a different angle on how to address solutions to this problem in your area?

10. Everybody has an opinion on Walmart. Invite reflection on the upside and downside of Walmart's presence in your community or entrance into urban areas. If possible, invite a Walmart employee to talk with your group about what it's like to work there. Discuss the difference that a Walmart has made in its neighborhood. Most importantly, make sure low-income workers are a part of this conversation.

11. Reflect on the sacrament of Communion as a vision for what God has called us to be and do vis-à-vis work. Then revisit the final quotation (from Doug Ottati) that closes this chapter. What strikes you most about it?

12. Finally, find out about groups in your area who are advocating for living wage jobs. The Service Employees International Union (www .seiu.org) will know about such groups. The SEIU can also respond to questions you may have about low-income work in this country. The Industrial Areas Foundation (www.industrialareasfoundation.org), the parent organization for WIN and BUILD, is also a good source of information. Then, after gathering the information you need, consider ways in which your congregation might get involved; then get involved!

Epilogue

The reflections in this volume are addressed to all who love and serve the city, bearing its daily stress, and are grounded in the conviction that the risen Lord *is* there, summoning us to join in at cruciform places where God is already at work, bringing life out of death. Our calling is to serve the sovereign cruciform God who is bringing abundance amid scarcity and resurrection from the graves of arrogance and diminution.

Blessings on your own journey until the day when we gather in the holy city, the new Jerusalem come down out of heaven from God. Until that day, Godspeed.

All Who Love and Serve Your City

All who love and serve your city,
all who bear its daily stress,
all who cry for peace and justice,
all who curse and all who bless:

In your day of wealth and plenty,
wasted work and wasted play,
call to mind the word of Jesus,
"You must work while it is day."

For all days are days of judgment,
and the Lord is waiting still,
drawing near a world that spurns him,
offering peace from Calvary's hill.

Risen Lord, shall yet the city
be the city of despair?
Come today, our judge, our glory;
Be its name, "The Lord is there!"[1]

Notes

INTRODUCTION

1. www.industrialareasfoundation.org/.

2. Roger Betsworth, *Social Ethics: An Examination of American Moral Traditions* (Louisville, KY: Westminster/John Knox Press, 1990), 110–11; Alan Taylor, "The New Jerusalem of the Early American Frontier," http://www.library.vanderbilt.edu/Quaderno/Quaderno5/Q5.C7.Taylor.pdf.

3. Ronald C. White, Jr., *A. Lincoln: A Biography* (New York: Random House, 2009), 377.

4. Serene Jones, *Trauma and Grace: Theology in a Ruptured World* (Louisville, KY: Westminster John Knox Press, 2009), 81.

5. Ernest Hemmingway, *A Farewell to Arms* (New York: Charles Scribner's Sons, 1957), 249.

6. I am indebted to Doug Ottati for this way of describing the effects of the cross. He says that through the lens of the cross we "discern the many Calvaries both great and small that clutter the horizons of our world." Douglas F. Ottati, *Jesus Christ and Christian Vision* (Louisville, KY: Westminster John Knox Press, 1995), 87.

7. Elizabeth A. Johnson, *Quest for the Living God: Mapping Frontiers in the Theology of God* (New York: Continuum Press, 2007), 55.

8. Theodore Jennings, *Transforming Atonement: A Political Theology of the Cross* (Minneapolis: Fortress Press, 2009), 214–15.

9. Ibid. (emphasis mine).

10. Ibid., 61.

11. Nadia Bolz-Weber, *Pastrix: The Cranky, Beautiful Faith of a Sinner and Saint* (New York: Jericho Books, 2013), 174.

12. Johnson, *Quest for the Living God*, 189–90.

13. Quoted in Ottati, *Jesus Christ and Christian Vision*, 135.

14. Ronald Peters, *Urban Ministry: An Introduction* (Nashville: Abingdon Press, 2007), 347–429.

15. Scott Greer, *The Emerging City: Myth and Reality* (New York: The Free Press of Glencoe, 1962), 98.

16. On the purpose of the church and its ministry see Douglas F. Ottati, *Reforming Protestantism: Christian Commitment in Today's World* (Minneapolis: Fortress Press, 1989), 94–99.

17. The inclusion of "mind" (*dianoia*) in Mark's version of the Great Commandment is thought to be a result of the Gospel's Hellenistic setting and "missionary outreach to thoughtful

Gentiles," and if so. I would argue that the life of the mind is also vital to ministry, especially in an urban setting. See M. Eugene Boring, *Mark: A Commentary*, New Testament Library (Louisville, KY: Westminster John Knox Press, 2006), 345.

18. The word "strength" (*ischyos*) can also be translated "power," so I will use this word in the modern sense as power in action or willpower.

19. "Heart" (*kardia*) in the Bible, can refer to the mind, but since the "mind" is already referenced in Mark's list of elements of the self, I take it that heart could also refer to the feelings or the inner self. So the way I will refer to "heart" in this book will emphasize the later. See Donald E. Gowan, ed. *The Westminster Theological Wordbook of the Bible* (Louisville, KY: Westminster John Knox Press, 2003), 328

20. "Soul" (*psychē*) can refer to the inner person but can also refer to the whole self. In this book, I will reference the soul as the integration of the whole self—heart, mind, and will—in loving God.

CHAPTER 1: THE STORY OF A GROCERY STORE

1. The racial makeup of the neighborhood was African American. Although most of the residents worked, they were also predominantly poor, inner-city folk. Our group of six from BUILD included both black and white folk, and while the churches we represented were in the neighborhood, most of us lived in more affluent parts of Baltimore.

2. http://thekojonnamdishow.org/off-mic/2010-07-07/closing-grocery-gap.

3. D.C. Hunger Solutions and Social Compact, *When Healthy Food Is Out of Reach: An Analysis of the Grocery Gap in the District of Columbia—2010*, http://www.dchunger.org/pdf/grocerygap.pdf, 3.

4. See The Mission Statement of the Baltimore City Food Policy Task Force (http://www.baltimorecity.gov/Government/AgenciesDepartments/Planning/FoodPolicyTaskForce.aspx and http://www.baltimorehealth.org/virtualsupermarket.html).

5. Gayraud S. Wilmore, "Theological Dimensions of Black Presbyterianism," *Periscope*, vol. 3, *African American Presbyterianism-Preparing for the 21st Century* (Louisville, KY: Racial Ethnic Ministry Unit, Presbyterian Church (U.S.A.), 1992), 3, 12.

6. H. Richard Niebuhr, *Radical Monotheism and Western Culture* (New York: Harper and Row, 1960), 37, 52. John Calvin says: "Sin is not our nature but its derangement." John Calvin, *Institutes of the Christian Religion*, ed. John T. McNeill, trans. Ford Lewis Battles (Philadelphia: Westminster Press, 1960), 2.1.10.

7. Walter Brueggemann, "The Litany of Abundance, the Myth of Scarcity," *Christian Century*, March 24–31, 1999, 342.

8. See Amy Jill-Levine, "Hermeneutics of Suspicion," in *Dictionary of Feminist Theologies*, ed. Letty Russell and Shannon Clarkson (Louisville, KY: Westminster John Knox Press, 1996), 140–41.

9. Douglas F. Ottati, *Reforming Protestantism: Christian Commitment in Today's World* (Louisville, KY: Westminster John Knox Press, 1995), chap. 5.

10. Ibid., 101.

11. Edward Chambers, *Roots for Radicals* (London: Continuum International Publishing Group Inc., 2003), 25.

12. Or the summary of the Torah: love the Lord your God with all your heart, soul, mind, and strength, and love your neighbor as yourself.

13. Sondra Wheeler, *What We Were Made For: Christian Reflections on Love* (San Francisco: Jossey-Bass, 2007), 112.

14. Ottati, *Reforming Protestantism*, 105.

15. Ibid., 108–9.

16. Langdon Gilkey, *On Niebuhr: A Theological Study* (Chicago: The University of Chicago Press, 2001), 35, 49.

17. Ottati, *Reforming Protestantism*, 112.

18. Ibid., 113.

19. Michael Gecan, *Effective Organizing for Congregational Renewal* (Skokie, IL: Acta Publications, 2008), 5–28. I commend this book to you for its more extensive explication of these tools and case studies of their application in congregational settings. For another explication of these tools see Ed Chambers's book *Roots for Radicals*, referenced earlier in this chapter.

20. Ottati, *Reforming Protestantism*, 101.

CHAPTER 2: CREATING COVENANT COMMUNITY

1. Hannah Arendt, *The Human Condition* (Chicago: The University of Chicago Press, 1958), 193.

2. Edward Chambers, *The Power of Relational Action* (Skokie, IL: Acta Publications, 2009), 12, 18.

3. Louise Green, "Sustainable Action: Planting the Seeds of Relational Organizing," http://www.uua.org/documents/greenlouise/seeds_relationalorg.pdf.

4. H. Richard Niebuhr, *Christ and Culture* (New York: Harper and Row, 1951), 103.

5. Ibid., 194.

6. Serene Jones, *Feminist Theory and Christian Theology: Cartographies of Grace* (Minneapolis: Augsburg Press, 2000), 121.

7. Ibid., 108–24.

8. Ibid., 61–68.

9. Chambers, *The Power of Relational Action*, 20.

10. Ibid., 11.

11. H. Richard Niebuhr, *The Responsible Self : An Essay in Christian Moral Philosophy*, Library of Theological Ethics (Louisville, KY: Westminster John Knox Press, 1999), 87.

12. Jeff Krehbiel, *Reflecting with Scripture on Community Organizing* (Chicago: Acta Publications, 2010).

13. See Ed Chambers's helpful discussion of the private and public in chap. 4 of *Roots for Radicals* (London: Continuum International Publishing Group Inc., 2003).

14. One of our members used a great image for the kind of questions one should ask in a relational meeting. She termed them "iceberg" questions, that is, questions that might invite someone to go deep under the surface.

15. Chambers, *The Power of the Relational Action*, 31.

CHAPTER 3: ENGAGING COVENANT COMMUNITY

1. Amy-Jill Levine, *The Misunderstood Jew: The Church and the Scandal of the Jewish Jesus* (San Francisco: Harper Collins, 2006), 23.

2. M. Eugene Boring, *Mark: A Commentary*, The New Testament Library (Louisville, KY: Westminster John Knox Press, 2006), 344.

3. Ernesto Cortes Jr., "A New Democratic Politics," http://swc2.hccs.edu/htmls/govdep/html/texsub/newdempolcp4.html.

4. Ibid.

5. Ibid.

6. H. Richard Niebuhr, *The Responsible Self : An Essay in Christian Moral Philosophy*, Library of Theological Ethics (Louisville, KY: Westminster John Knox Press, 1999), 87.

7. I owe a debt of gratitude to Mark Greiner and the good folk of Takoma Park Presbyterian Church in Maryland for the initial idea of doing a listening campaign. Although New York Avenue's campaign was structured differently from Takoma Park's, their questions formed the basis for our own.

8. Richard Horsley, *Jesus and Empire: The Kingdom of God and the New World Disorder* (Minneapolis: Fortress Press, 2003), 20, 21.

9. Bethany McLean and Joe Nocera, *All the Devils Are Here: The Hidden History of The Financial Crisis* (New York: Portfolio/Penguin, 2010), from the book jacket.

10. Brian Blount, *Revelation: A Commentary*, The New Testament Library (Louisville, KY: Westminster John Knox Press, 2009), 41.

11. Ibid., 48, 49.

12. Rowan Williams, *Christ on Trial* (Grand Rapids: Eerdmans, 2000), 6, 52, 69.

13. Jeffrey Stout, *Blessed Are the Organized: Grassroots Democracy in America* (Princeton, NJ: Princeton University Press, 2010), 279–80.

14. Peter J. Paris, "The Theology and Ethics of Martin Luther King Jr.," in *Reformed Theology for the Third Christian Millennium: The 2001 Sprunt Lectures*, ed B. A. Gerrish (Louisville, KY: Westminster John Knox Press, 2003), 41.

15. Doug Hostetter, "Neighbors in the Bosnian Tragedy," in *Transforming Violence Linking Local and Global Peacemaking,* ed. Robert Herr and Judy Zimmerman Herr (Waterloo, ON: Herald Press, 1998), 105–6, 109.

Quoted in Susan Brooks Thistlethwaite, ed., *Interfaith Just Peacemaking; Jewish, Christian, and Muslim Perspectives on the New Paradigm of Peace and War* (New York: Palgrave Macmillan, 2011), 34–35.

16. Ibid.

CHAPTER 4: DEEPENING COVENANT COMMUNITY

1. Wendy Farley, *The Wounding and Healing of Desire: Weaving Heaven and Earth* (Louisville, KY: Westminster John Knox Press: 2005), 10.

2. Reinhold Niebuhr, *The Nature and Destiny of Man, Vol. I*, Library of Theological Ethics (Louisville, KY: Westminster John Knox Press, 1996), 183.

3. Farley, *Wounding*, 58–60.

4. Paul Ricoeur, *Oneself as Another*, trans. Kathleen Blamey (Chicago: The University of Chicago Press, 1992), 193–94.

5. Richard John Neuhaus, "Commencement and Causes." Commencement address recorded at Union Theological Seminary, Richmond, Virginia, May 25, 1980. Sound recording is in the collection of the William Smith Morton Library at Union Presbyterian Seminary, Richmond, Virginia.

6. Farley, *Wounding*, xviii, 116.

7. Ibid., 116.

8. Marjorie Thompson, *Soul Feast: An Invitation to the Christian Spiritual Life* (Louisville, KY: Westminster John Knox Press, 2005), 146.

9. Ibid.

CHAPTER 5: TEACHING MOMENTS

1. Douglas Ottati, *Theology for Liberal Protestants* (Grand Rapids: Eerdmans, 2013), 3.

2. Edwin Friedman, *Generation to Generation: Family Process in Church and Synagogue* (New York: Guildford Press, 2011), loc 48 of the Kindle edition.

3. Walter Wink, "Jesus and Alinsky," http://www.commondreams.org/views04/1216-30.htm.

4. H. Richard Niebuhr, *Christ and Culture*, 103.

5. Ibid., 108.

6. Pages 20–21. See also notes 11–14 in chapter 1.

7. Walker Percy, *The Second Coming* (New York: Farrar, Straus and Giroux, 1980), 16.

8. Ibid.

9. Thomas Merton, *New Seeds of Contemplation* (New York: New Directions, 1961), 29.

10. Farley further explores this problem by calling attention to an aspect of Augustine's *The City of God* that I had never noticed before. The standard interpretation of Augustine is that the human fall into sin was rooted in the arrogance of Adam, who sought to be like God. What Farley notes, however, is that for Augustine, the fall actually began with angels who fell from heaven because of "a moment of panic, a kind of existential terror when they realized that they could be separated from the love of God. This moment of panic was such that it turned their attention from God to themselves and this constituted the fall that propelled Satan out of paradise and filled the world with demons intent on our destruction." So, according to Farley's interpretation of Augustine, the deepest root of our self-absorption is not pride but pain—"the intensity of . . . our fears, disappointments, sufferings, grief too great for us to bear"—grief that we experience as a loss of love. Wendy Farley, *The Wounding and Healing of Desire: Weaving Heaven and Earth* (Louisville, KY: Westminster John Knox Press, 2005), 33.

11. Ibid., 163–64.

12. Ibid., 160.

13. Sandra M. Schneiders, *Written That You May Believe: Encountering Jesus in the Fourth Gospel* (New York: Crossroad Publishing, 2000), 170–72.

14. Justo L. González, *The Apostles' Creed for Today* (Louisville, KY: Westminster John Knox Press, 2007), 2–3.

15. Gail R. O'Day, "The Gospel of John," in *The New Interpreter's Bible*, vol. 9 (Nashville: Abingdon, 1995), 744–45.

16. Ibid.

17. David Rensberger, "Sectarianism and Theological Interpretation in John," *"What Is John?": Literary and Social Readings of the Fourth Gospel*, vol. 2, ed. Fernando F. Segovia (Atlanta: Society of Biblical Literature, 1998), 145–46.

18. John Calvin, *Institutes of the Christian Religion* 2.13.4; ed. John T. Mc Neill, trans. Ford Lewis Battles (Philadelphia: Westminster Press, 1960).

19. Douglas F. Ottati, *Hopeful Realism: Reclaiming the Poetry of Theology* (Cleveland: Pilgrim Press, 1999), 69–84.

20. R. Alan Culpepper, "The Gospel of John as a Document of Faith in a Pluralistic Culture," in *"What Is John?": Readers and Readings of the Fourth Gospel*, ed. Fernando F. Segovia (Atlanta: Scholars Press, 1996), 123–24.

21. Theodore Jennings, *Transforming Atonement: A Political Theology of the Cross* (Minneapolis: Fortress Press, 2009), 58.

22. Michael Walzer, *Thick and Thin: Moral Argument at Home and Abroad* (Notre Dame, IN: University of Notre Dame Press, 1994), 8; quoted in Eric Mount Jr., *Covenant, Community, and the Common Good: An Interpretation of Christian Ethics* (Cleveland: The Pilgrim Press, 1999), 18.

CHAPTER 6: TALKING ABOUT RACE AND POVERTY IN THE CITY

1. Raymond E. Brown, *The Birth of the Messiah: A Commentary on the Infancy Narratives in Matthew and Luke* (Garden City, NY: Doubleday, 1977), 197.

2. Mark Alan Powell, *Chasing the Eastern Star: Adventures in Biblical Reader-Response Criticism* (Louisville, KY: Westminster John Knox Press, 2001), 138–47.

3. See Stephen R. Haynes, *Noah's Curse: The Biblical Justification of American Slavery* (New York: Oxford University Press, 2002).

4. See Marc Saperstein, *Moments of Crisis in Jewish-Christian Relations* (Valley Forge, PA: Trinity Press International, 1989).

5. J. Kameron Carter, *Race: A Theological Account* (New York: Oxford University Press, 2008), 11–36.

6. Jonathan Tran, "The New Black Theology," *Christian Century* (February 8, 2012): 25. Boldface mine, for spoken emphasis.

7. Ibid., 24–25.

8. Cone, *The Cross and the Lynching Tree*, 165–66.

9. Roger Betsworth, *Social Ethics: An Examination of American Moral Traditions* (Louisville, KY: Westminster/John Knox Press, 1990), 110–11.

10. Ronald C. White Jr., *A. Lincoln: A Biography* (New York: Random House, 2009), 377.

11. Carter, *Race*, 147.

12. Quoted in *Death: A Source Book about Christian Death*, ed. Virginia Sloyan (Chicago: Liturgy Training Publications, 1990), 49.

13. Cone, *The Cross and the Lynching Tree*, 22–23.

14. Ibid., 41.

15. James Cone, "Theology's Great Sin: Silence in the Face of White Supremacy," *Union Seminary Quarterly Review* 55 (2001): 1–14.

16. Michelle Alexander, *The New Jim Crow: Mass Incarceration in the Age of Colorblindness* (New York: The New Press, 2010), 2, 6–7.

17. Ibid., 242.

18. R. Alan Culpepper, "Luke," in *The New Interpreter's Bible*, vol. 9, ed. Leander E. Keck, et al. (Nashville: Abingdon, 1995), 106.

19. Ted Hiebert, "The Tower of Babel and the Origin of the World's Cultures," *Journal of Biblical Literature* 126 (2007): 29–58; see also *Christian Century* 124/16 (August 7, 2007): 11.

20. Tammerie Day, *Constructing Solidarity for a Liberative Ethic: Anti-Racism, Action, and Justice* (New York: Palgrave Macmillan, 2012), 4–5.

CHAPTER 7: JOBS IN THE URBAN CONTEXT

1. Paul Osterman and Beth Shulman, *Good Jobs America: Making Work Better for Everyone* (New York: Russell Sage Foundation, 2011), 24–25.

2. Arthur Herman, *How the Scots Invented the Modern World* (New York: Three Rivers Press, 2001), 216.

3. Ibid., 219–20.

4. Robert C. Solomon, *Ethics and Excellence: Cooperation and Integrity in Business* (New York: Oxford University Press, 1992), 148.

5. Ibid., 150.

6. Osterman and Shulman, *Good Jobs America*, 24–25.

7. See the first question of the Westminster Shorter Catechism.

8. Douglas F. Ottati, "Recovering Faithfulness in Our Callings," in *Spiritual Traditions for the Contemporary Church*, ed. Robin Maas and Gabriel O'Donnell (Nashville: Abingdon, 1990), 222.

9. Douglas F. Ottati, *Reforming Protestantism: Christian Commitment in Today's World* (Louisville, KY: Westminster John Knox Press, 1995), 118.

10. Ibid., 142.

11. *The Diane Rehm Show*, November 17, 2011.

12. Theodore W. Jennings Jr., *Loyalty to God: The Apostles' Creed in Life and Liturgy* (Nashville: Abingdon Press, 1992), 213.

13. Ibid., 214.

14. Osterman and Shulman, *Good Jobs America*, 144.

15. Ibid., 134, 140, 144.

16. Christopher H. Evans and William R. Herzog II, *The Faith of 50 Million: Baseball, Religion, and American Culture* (Louisville, KY: Westminster John Knox Press, 2002), 36–44.

17. Mark Allan Powell, *What Do They Hear? Bridging the Gap between Pulpit and Pew* (Nashville: Abingdon, 2007), 11–27.

18. Christine Dugas, "Study Shows Racial Wealth Gap Continues to Widen," *USA Today*, http://www.usatoday.com/story/money/personalfinance/2013/02/27/racial-wealth -gap-growing/1948899/ and http://dcentric.wamu.org/2011/07/racial-wealth-gap-reaches -historic-levels/index.html.

19. See Stacey Detwiler, *Staying Green: Strategies to Improve Operations and Maintenance of Green Infrastructure in the Chesapeake Bay Watershed*, http://www.americanrivers .org/assets/pdfs/reports-and-publications/staying-green-strategies-improve-operations-and -maintenance.pdf.

20. Jeremy Rifkin, *The End of Work: The Decline of the Global Labor Force and the Dawn of the Post-Market Era* (New York: G. P. Putnam's Sons, 1995), xv.

21. See Detwiler, *Staying Green*, http://www.americanrivers.org/assets/pdfs/reports -and-publications/staying-green-and-growing-jobs.pdf.

22. *Washington Post* (July 14, 2013), C6.

23. See the online *Forbes* article on how a McDonald's worker lives on a minimum wage: Laura Shin, "How She Lives on Minimum Wage: One McDonald's Worker's Budget," http://www.forbes.com/sites/laurashin/2013/07/19/how-she-lives-on -minimum-wage-one-mcdonalds-workers-budget/.

24. http://www.pbs.org/newshour/bb/business/july-dec13/wages_07-17.html.

25. Matt Miller, "30 Million Workers Need a Raise," *Washington Post*, op-ed, February 9, 2013.

26. Paul Galbreath, *Leading from the Table* (Herdon, VA: Alban Institute, 2008), 39.

27. Ibid., 4.

28. Ottati, *Reforming Protestantism*, 113.

29. Osterman and Shulman, *Good Jobs America*, 144.

EPILOGUE

1. Eric Routley, "All Who Love and Serve Your City," in *Glory to God: The Presbyterian Hymnal* (Louisville, KY: Westminster John Knox Press, 2013), #351. Used by permission of Hope Publishing Company.

CPSIA information can be obtained at www.ICGtesting.com
Printed in the USA
LVOW11s1729140515

438540LV00013B/246/P